HKP SPORT SCIENCE MONOGRAPH SERIES
Volume 3

Growth and Fitness of Flemish Girls

The Leuven Growth Study

Jan Simons, PhD
Gaston P. Beunen, PhD
Roland Renson, PhD
Albrecht L.M. Claessens, PhD
Bart Vanreusel, PhD
Johan Lefevre, PhD
Catholic University of Leuven
Editors

Human Kinetics Books
Champaign, Illinois

Library of Congress Cataloging-in-Publication Data

Growth and fitness of Flemish girls : the Leuven Growth Study / Jan Simons . . . [et al.]. eds.
p. cm. -- (HKP sport science monograph series, ISSN 0894-4229 ; v. 3)
Includes bibliographical references.
ISBN 0-87322-284-9
1. Girls--Belgium--Flanders--Growth. 2. Girls--Health and hygiene--Belgium--Flanders. 3. Teenage girls--Belgium--Flanders--Growth. 4. Teenage girls--Health and hygiene--Belgium--Flanders. I. Simons, Jan, 1932- . II. Series.
RJ144.G76 1990
613'.04242'094933--dc20 90-4044
CIP

ISBN: 0-87322-284-9

ISSN: 0894-4229

Developmental Editor: Kathy Kane
Assistant Editor: Timothy Ryan
Proofreader: Phaedra Hargis
Production Director: Ernie Noa
Typesetters: Cindy Pritchard, Sandra Meier
Text Layout: Denise Lowry
Printer: Versa Press

Printed in the United States of America

10 9 8 7 6 5 4 3 2 1

Human Kinetics Books
A Division of Human Kinetics Publishers, Inc.
Box 5076, Champaign, IL 61825-5076
1-800-747-4HKP

Contents

HKP Sport Science Monograph Series

Ten years ago I completed a series of studies on competitive anxiety that validated the Sport Competition Anxiety Test (SCAT). I wanted to publish all this work in one place rather than chopping it into shorter research articles that would meet the space restrictions of scholarly journals. Because a place to publish monograph-length research did not exist then in the sport sciences, I published it as the third book of the then neophyte Human Kinetics Publishers.

The need for a research monograph series continues today and was brought back to my attention by Professor Robert Malina when he sought to have the cumulative work of *Physical Growth and Motor Performance of Belgian Boys Followed Longitudinally Between 12 and 18 Years of Age* published in its entirety. The report of that project was the first publication in the new *HKP Sport Science Monograph Series*. The series is an extension of Human Kinetics Publishers' scholarly journal program.

The *HKP Sport Science Monograph Series* is another endeavor to provide a useful communication channel for recording extensive research programs by sport scientists. Many publishers have discontinued publishing monographs because they have proven uneconomical. It is my hope that with the cooperation of authors, the use of electronic support systems, and the purchase of these monographs by sport scientists and libraries we can continue this series over the years.

The series will publish original research reports and reviews of literature that are sufficiently extensive not to lend themselves to reporting in available research journals. Subject matter pertinent both to the broad fields of the sport sciences and to physical education are considered appropriate for the monograph series, especially research in

- Sport biomechanics,
- Sport physiology,
- Motor behavior (including motor control and learning, motor development, and adapted physical activity),
- Sport psychology,
- Sport sociology, and
- Sport pedagogy.

Authors who wish to publish in the monograph series should submit two copies of the complete manuscript to the publisher. All manuscripts must conform to the current *APA Publication Manual* and be of a length between 120 and 300 doublespaced manuscript pages. The manuscript will be sent to two reviewers who will follow a review process similar to that used for scholarly journals. The decision with regard to the manuscript's acceptability will be based on its judged contribution to knowledge and on economic feasibility. Publications that are accepted, after all required revisions are made, must be submitted to the publisher on computer disk for electronic transfer to typesetting. No royalties will be paid for monographs published in this series.

Authors wishing to submit a manuscript to the monograph series or desiring further information should write to: Monograph Editor, Human Kinetics Publishers, Box 5076, Champaign, IL 61825 for further details.

Rainer Martens

Preface

With this monograph, another phase in the physical fitness research tradition of the Study Center for Physical Development has been finished. This tradition dates back 50 years to the foundation of the Institute of Physical Education at the K.U. Leuven. In the late 1940s and early 1950s a concern for more individualized physical education in the schools was brought to our attention by Binet and Hébert in Europe and by Brace and McCloy in the U.S.A. Individualized physical education requires the construction of homogeneous groups, for which standardized measuring instruments are needed.

Also, in the sports medical center of the Institute, attempts were made to introduce some tests in order to evaluate the physical performance capacities of sportspersons. In the beginning, only endurance-type tests were included. In Leuven, the Harvard step test and Brouha index were introduced shortly after World War II, whereas in other centers older heart rate recovery tests such as the Martinet and Schneider tests were still in use. Gradually test batteries measuring several motor fitness factors were adopted and, from 1957 through the next 10 years, an abbreviated version (step test, situp, and vertical jump) of the U.S. Naval Aviation Physical Fitness test was used.

From all these tests it appeared that Belgian youngsters had endurance capacities comparable to their age peers of other countries, but their motor performance capacities were clearly inferior. Great was our surprise when American physical educationists claimed that the fitness level of American youth was poor as compared to the Europeans! Furthermore, Americans were able to convince their president, John Kennedy, to start a fitness program for American youth.

It was clear that the measured fitness level depended on the tests included in the test battery and that, in this respect, there was need for an instrument that was adapted for Belgian youth. Consequently, the Study Center for Physical Development was founded in 1967, and large epidemiological fitness studies were initiated. In the first stage, a combined longitudinal and cross-sectional investigation on 21,000 boys was conducted (Ostyn, Simons, Beunen, Renson, & Van Gerven, 1980; Beunen, Malina, Van't Hof, Simons, Ostyn, Renson, & Van Gerven, 1988). In the second stage, a cross-sectional study on 9,940 girls aged 6 through 18 years was carried out. In both projects physical fitness was operationalized in a broad sense, including a somatic component, a cardiovascular–motor component, and a behavioral component, the daily physical activity. This concept was then approached from a developmental, a differential, and a sociocultural perspective. Both projects were preceded by a pilot study in which the reliability, validity, objectivity, and standardization of the tests and measurements were thoroughly investigated. This investigation has led to the construction of our own test batteries.

The present monograph reports the results of the Leuven Growth Study of Flemish Girls. A detailed description of the pilot study and research design is given, with special attention to the data quality control. In our opinion, such a monograph gives the unique opportunity to describe important aspects of the total project in detail. The major part of the manuscript deals with growth patterns in somatic dimensions, biological maturation, physical performance characteristics, and sports participation of the girls. Furthermore, the sociocultural characteristics of the sample are described, and examples of practical tools for the evaluation of the physical fitness level of individuals or groups are included. This monograph is unique in that it covers, in one volume, a wide variation in growth and development of human characteristics, based on a large representative sample of a whole population assembled by the same team of 12 instructors under the supervision of experienced kinanthropometrists.

Michel Ostyn, MD

Acknowledgments

We would like to thank Prof. Dr. M. Ostyn, who was the initiator and director of the Leuven Growth Study of Belgian Boys during which our concept of physical fitness and the tools that were used to measure this concept were first established. The present study is highly indebted to his pioneering. Furthermore, we gratefully acknowledge the valuable contributions of the test instructors and research assistants who collected the data and prepared the computer files: Mrs. T. Bruyneel, R. Colla, A. Colpaert, D. De Cooman, K. Den Haerynck, N. Desmet, R. De Smet, J. Elskens, A.-M. Fobelets, H. Leclercq, G. Luyten, J. Massy, O. Moria, C. Schueremans, G. Schueremans, S. Van Tomme, G. Vandeput, G. Vandermeersch, M. Van Esser, C. Van Maercke, and C. Vercammen, and Messrs. Dr. M. Buekers, W. De Vroye, C. Overbeke, Dr. H. Smulders, J. Uyttebrouck, E. Van Cauteren, and Dr. D. Van Gool.

We are also indebted to numerous graduate students for their enthusiastic cooperation in this project. Special thanks are also extended to the Bureaus of Statistics and Planning of the Ministry of Education (Nationale Opvoeding) and of the National Secretariat of Catholic Schools (Nationaal Secretariaat van het Katholiek Onderwijs), more specifically to Dr. Jur. A. Van Den Bosch. We are also indebted to the technical and administrative staff of our Institute for their willingness to help us at any time, especially to S. Teck for her patience and perseverance in dealing with numerous manuscripts. Finally we would like to thank the sponsors, the directors, the physical educators, and the pupils of the 88 primary and secondary schools. Financial support was given by the Ministry of Labour and Employment, the Belgian Olympic Interfederal Committee, and Siemens n.v.

J. Simons
G.P. Beunen
R. Renson
A.L.M. Claessens
B. Vanreusel
J.A.V. Lefevre

Chapter 1

The Study Design

Jan Simons, Gaston P. Beunen, Roland Renson, and Dirk Van Gerven

The Pilot Study

In 1967 the Leuven Growth Study of Belgian Boys started with a pilot study. The purpose of this study was to select valid and reliable tests and measurements for the main study. Factor analyses were used to detect the underlying dimensions of motor fitness and body structure and to select the best measurements for the different dimensions. In the area of motor fitness this resulted in the construction of a battery of tests for boys (see Table 1.1).

A complete overview has been given by Simons et al. (1968-1969, 1969, 1970). Since it was also intended to investigate the physical fitness of Flemish

Table 1.1 Motor Test Battery for Boys Aged 12-19 Years

Factors	Tests
1. Functional strength	Bent arm hang
2. Static strength	Arm pull dynamometer
3. Explosive strength	Vertical jump
4. Trunk strength	Leg lifts
5. Flexibility	Sit and reach
6. Running speed	50-m shuttle run
7. Speed of limb movement	Plate tapping
8. Balance	Stick balance
9. Cardiorespiratory recovery	1-min step test

girls aged 6 to 19 years, the problem of the existing basic dimensions and the selection of appropriate tests was raised again. A new pilot study was therefore carried out on a limited group of girls during the academic year 1974-1975.

Method

After examining the factor analytic studies of motor fitness in the literature, nine physical fitness factors were hypothesized. For eight of these factors, several tests were selected. In Table 1.2, the different factors and the 24 selected tests are listed. The ninth factor, cardiorespiratory endurance, is not included in this pilot study because of practical considerations. However, its existence has been clearly demonstrated. The sample included 402 girls, aged 11 to 19 years. The subjects

Table 1.2 Reliability Coefficients of the Selected Motor Tests in the Three Age Groups

Factors	Tests	Age (years) 11-13 $n = 65$	14-15 $n = 139$	16-19 $n = 173$
1. Static strength	Arm pull dynamometer	.84	.84	.86
	Handgrip	.81	.86	.75
	Medicine ball put	.81	.84	.75
2. Functional strength	Bent arm hang	.91	.82	.86
	Modified push-ups	.83	.77	.70
3. Explosive strength	Vertical jump	.79	.76	.79
	Standing broad jump	.91	.92	.88
	Basketball throw	.87	.81	.80
4. Trunk strength	Leg lifts	.81	.79	.68
	Sit-ups	.85	.87	.80
	Leg raiser	.82	.80	.69
5. Running speed	Shuttle run 50 m	.81	.81	.78
	Dodge run	.83	.88	.78
	Shuttle run 40 m	.84	.78	.70
	Figure 8-duck	.74	.76	.76
6. Speed of limb movement	Plate tapping	.82	.73	.80
	1-foot tapping	.87	.80	.83
	Vertical plate tapping	.72	.73	.72
7. Flexibility	Sit and reach	.93	.94	.94
	Ankle flexiblity	.67	.67	.62
	Trunk rotation	.84	.86	.85
8. Balance	1-foot lengthwise balance	.69	.61	.66
	Flamingo balance	.83	.79	.85
	Stick balance	.55	.77	.72

were subsequently divided into three age-groups (11-13, 14-15, and 16-19 years). The 24 tests were administered to all subjects twice, with an interval of one week between them.

Results and Discussion

In each age group, the test–retest reliability of the tests was calculated (Pearson product-moment coefficient). The results of this reliability study also appear in Table 1.2. Almost all the tests have a sufficient reliability in the three age groups. With a few exceptions the coefficients for all tests scored above .80.

In each age group and in the total group, a factor analysis was carried out according to the maximum likelihood procedure, followed by orthogonal and oblique rotations using the Varimax and the Oblimin criteria (see Table 1.3). In

Table 1.3 Factor Analysis: Total Group
N = 402 (Maximum Likehood—Varimax—Oblimin)

Factors	Tests	I	II	III	IV	V	VI	VII
1. Static strength	Arm pull dynamometer	.73	.21	.17	.17	.32	.13	.12
	Handgrip	.77	.08	.13	.18	.35	.00	.09
	Medicine ball put	.65	.30	.22	.39	.21	.17	.36
2. Functional strength	Bent arm hang	.10	.60	.45	.48	.19	.24	.30
	Modified push-ups	.23	.60	.38	.39	.06	.11	.35
3. Explosive strength	Vertical jump	.32	.32	.71	.48	.19	.24	.30
	Standing broad jump	.41	.44	.71	.62	.20	.34	.33
	Basketball throw	.71	.28	.20	.41	.17	.30	.39
4. Trunk strength	Leg lifts	.17	.68	.28	.34	.17	.27	.24
	Sit-ups	.19	.53	.34	.50	.09	.22	.36
	Leg raiser	.19	.65	.08	.22	.01	.15	.21
5. Running speed	Shuttle run 50 m	.28	.40	.35	.80	.26	.22	.34
	Dodge run	.41	.36	.31	.81	.30	.27	.35
	Shuttle run 40 m	.36	.44	.46	.78	.26	.30	.37
	Figure 8-duck	.21	.39	.45	.65	.19	.43	.34
6. Speed of limb movement	Plate tapping	.48	.16	.16	.37	.72	.09	.43
	1-foot tapping	.39	.38	.21	.51	.48	.24	.37
	Vertical plate tapping	.37	.07	.19	.28	.67	.20	.25
7. Flexibility	Sit and reach	.28	.25	.16	.15	.19	.57	.17
	Ankle flexibility	.02	.06	.03	.11	.05	.44	.10
	Trunk rotation	.06	.23	.27	.26	.00	.62	.19
8. Balance	1-foot lengthwise balance	.05	.28	.17	.25	.09	.17	.56
	Flamingo balance	.17	.38	.32	.41	.25	.23	.58
	Stick balance	.23	.10	.07	.16	.17	.11	.48

the four factor analyses, seven oblique factors were extracted. The rotated factor loadings obtained from the analysis of the total group are shown in this table.

The extracted factors were interpreted as follows:

Factor I: Arm pull dynamometer, handgrip, medicine ball put, and basketball throw showed the highest saturations for this factor. Three of these tests are known to be measurements of static strength. The basketball throw was selected as a measure of explosive strength, but has in fact its highest loading on Factor I. The latter was identified as *static strength.*

Factor II: All the selected tests for the functional and trunk strength factors had loadings on Factor II. No separate factors for functional strength and trunk strength could be identified. This is very similar to the results in our factor analyses of boys of 12 and 13 years of age. It seems that for girls, all strength tests in which subjects must perform against their body weight have loadings on one factor, which can be termed *functional strength.* Quite often this factor is also called local muscular endurance or dynamic strength, referring to the supposed underlying physiological mechanisms that limit the performance in tests that measure this capacity.

Factor III: Vertical jump and standing broad jump clearly have high saturations for Factor III, which can be described as *explosive strength.*

Factor IV: In spite of the fact that a few other tests have some saturations for Factor IV, the tests for the measurements of running speed clearly have the highest loadings. Factor IV can thus be identified as a *speed* factor.

Factor V: Plate tapping, vertical plate tapping, and in a lesser degree one-foot tapping, have substantial loadings on Factor V. This factor can logically be called a *limb speed* factor.

Factor VI: This factor can best be termed *flexibility* because the tests selected for that purpose show the highest loadings.

Factor VII: *Balance* seems here to be the best denominator because all the balance tests have the highest saturations for this dimension.

The intercorrelations between the oblique factors are given in Table 1.4. It should be noted that these factors have only a slight degree of interrelationship.

Table 1.4 Intercorrelation of Oblique Factors—Total Group N = 402

Factors	I	II	III	IV	V	VI	VII
I	1.00	.10	−.02	.12	.30	−.02	.09
II		1.00	.17	−.18	.04	.12	−.14
III			1.00	.22	.05	−.08	.06
IV				1.00	−.04	.11	−.25
V					1.00	.04	−.07
VI						1.00	.10
VII							1.00

Therefore, it can be concluded that the identified factors are, for the most part, independent dimensions of the motor ability of girls.

The comparison between the factor analyses of adolescent boys and girls leads to the conclusion that the structure of motor ability is highly similar in both sexes. In both males and females, there are seven common factors, namely static, functional, and explosive strength, running speed, speed of limb movement, balance, and flexibility. The balance factor, which was not so clearly isolated in the analyses of Belgian boys, was easily identified in the factor analyses of girls. The selected balance tests showed a relatively high degree of reliability, especially the modified, one-foot lengthwise balance test (flamingo balance), which was not the case in the pilot study on adolescent boys (Ostyn, Simons, Beunen, Renson & Van Gerven, 1980).

Nevertheless, we observed some differences. In the analyses of older boys there is a clear-cut separation of measures of functional and trunk strength. This separation was not found in the results for 12- and 13-year-old boys, nor in those of girls 12 to 19 years of age. The existence of a cardiorespiratory endurance factor as a separate dimension of physical fitness in boys and girls has been demonstrated.

A separate study was undertaken to find a reliable and valid measurement for this dimension. Boys and girls aged 12 to 19 years were tested on a battery of short and longer running events. Factor analyses proved clearly that a 480-m shuttle run is an appropriate indoor test for the measurement of cardiorespiratory endurance. On the other hand, the pulse frequency after a standardized step test and the pulse frequency during a standardized bicycle ergometer test proved to measure different aspects of the underlying physiological mechanisms (Van Gerven & Vanden Eynde, 1978). In conclusion we can state that there is a substantial relationship between the basic dimensions of motor ability in Belgian boys and girls 12 to 19 years of age.

A final step in the pilot study consisted of selecting the tests for the measurement of the different factors. For each factor a test was selected that showed not

Table 1.5 Selected Motor Test Battery

Factors	Tests	Mean reliability coefficients of the three age groups	Mean factor loadings of the three age groups
1. Static strength	Arm pull	.85	.73
2. Functional strength	Bent arm hang	.87	.60
3. Explosive strength	Stand. broad jump	.91	.71
4. Running speed	Shuttle run 50 m	.80	.80
5. Speed of limb movement	Plate tapping	.79	.72
6. Flexibility	Sit and reach	.94	.57
7. Balance	Flamingo balance	.83	.58
8. Endurance	Shuttle run 480 m	—	.90

only a high saturation on that factor but also a high reliability. The selected test series, consisting of eight tests, is presented in Table 1.5. It can be observed that the tests have a fairly good reliability and are clearly a measure of the different factors. The comparison between the motor test series in boys and girls leads to the conclusion that, by and large, they measure the same dimension by the same test. There are a few exceptions, however. The vertical jump was used as a measure of explosive strength in boys, whereas the standing broad jump proved to be the best test for girls, although it can be replaced by the vertical jump. Stick balance was selected for boys. As a measure of the balance factor for girls, the flamingo balance is proposed. Finally, there was no need for a test to measure trunk strength in girls since trunk strength was not identified as a separate factor.

The Selection of Tests and Measurements

Physical fitness is a highly complex phenomenon in which a number of factors influence one another. This conclusion was clearly formulated in the Leuven Growth Study of Belgian Boys (Ostyn et al., 1980). Physical fitness may be considered as the result of the combined action of somatic, motor, cardiorespiratory, and behavioral components. What is more, these interactions are best examined from a variety of standpoints. Developmental, differential, and sociocultural approaches all provide new and useful information. Figure 1.1 represents in schematic fashion the operational determination of physical fitness, as the concept is understood in this study. In the following section the selection of tests and measurements in various contexts will be discussed in detail.

Motor Ability Tests

One of the major objectives of the Leuven Growth Study of Flemish Girls was to generate comparative data relative to the physical fitness of boys and girls. This aim could only be achieved if in both investigations identical tests and measurements were used. In the discussion of the pilot study (see beginning of this chapter), the method of constructing a battery of motor ability tests for girls aged 12 to 19 years was explained. In this investigation, it was found that the motor characteristics of boys and girls are highly similar, and that most of the relevant factors can be measured by the same tests. It was accordingly decided to retain the battery of tests from the boys' study for use in the growth study on girls. The measurement of explosive strength was carried out by means of the vertical jump test instead of the standing broad jump. Although functional trunk strength did not emerge as a separate factor in girls, the leg lift test was nevertheless retained in the test battery. Lastly, for the measurement of balance, the more reliable and valid flamingo balance test was chosen instead of the stick balance test.

Considering that girls are characterized by earlier growth and development than boys, it was decided to extend the age range to 6 to 19 years. At the start of the main study, the applicability of the battery of tests was tested on girls aged 6 to 12 years. It turned out that for certain factors, the selected tests were not appropriate for girls in the first three grades of primary school. In these girls, explosive strength was measured using the standing broad jump and functional

DEVELOPMENTAL APPROACH

PHYSICAL FITNESS

PHYSICAL MATURITY

BODY SIZE

BODY PROPORTION

BODY COMPOSITION

BODY TYPE

MOTOR ABILITY

CARDIO - RESPIRATORY ENDURANCE

PHYSICAL ACTIVITY

SPORT SKILL

HEALTH KNOWLEDGE

DIFFERENTIAL APPROACH

SOCIOCULTURAL APPROACH

Figure 1.1. Schematic representation of the operational definition of physical fitness and the different approaches.

trunk strength with the sit-ups test. In addition, for the measurement of balance, the flamingo balance test was performed with a wider foot support. The test battery that was finally used is summarized in Table 1.6.

Body Size, Body Proportion, Somatotype, and Maturity Characteristics

The selection of anthropometric measurements was based on various criteria. A survey was made of the existing literature dealing with body structure and using factor-analytic methods (Simons & Van Gerven, 1970-1971; Van Gerven, 1976;

Table 1.6 Motor Ability Tests Used in the Leuven Growth Study of Flemish Girls

Factors	Tests
Static strength	Arm pull
Functional strength	Bent arm hang
Explosive strength	Vertical jump (starting from 4th grade)
	Standing broad bump (1st till 3rd grade)
Trunk strength	Leg lifts (starting from 4th grade)
	Sit-ups (1st till 3rd grade)
Running speed	Shuttle run 50 m
Speed of limb movement	Plate tapping
Flexibility	Sit and reach
Balance	Flamingo balance

Beunen & Van Hellemont, 1980). In these investigations, reference is made to a fat factor, a bone length growth factor including trunk and limbs as two subfactors, a muscle factor, a bone breadth growth factor in respect to the bones, and a breadth development factor relating to the total body structure. Furthermore, it appears that head, hands, and feet are characterized by a structure that is relatively independent of that of the trunk and the limbs. Secondly, the selection of anthropometric variables adopted in the boys' study was also taken into account, and most measurements were again selected in order to allow comparisons between the sexes.

Furthermore, all measurements necessary for the calculations involved in the anthropometric somatotype technique of Heath–Carter were also selected (Carter, 1975). In comparison with the boys' study, the number of anthropometric indicators was expanded by three head measurements. In addition to bodily measurements, three standard photographs were taken in order to calculate the trunk index (Sheldon, Lewis, & Tenney, 1969) and, if possible, to devise a new typology for girls. A photograph of the foot sole with the subject in the normal standing position was taken as well. The purpose of this procedure was to allow the detection of possible pathological deviations as well as to be able to add a number of anthropometric measurements of the feet to the existing data.

As in all major growth studies it was decided to include estimations of the biological maturation process in the testing procedures. Age at menarche was recorded using the retrospective as well as the status quo procedure and skeletal age was assessed according to the TWII method (Tanner, Whitehouse, Cameron, Marshall, Healy, & Goldstein, 1983). Although it would have been interesting to have more information on sexual development, such as breast and pubic hair development, it was decided that the testing procedure in which entire school classes were measured and tested in one session did not allow nude photographs or complete undressing of the subjects. It was anticipated that the inclusion of these techniques would lead to a number of refusals that could have endangered

Table 1.7 Somatic Characteristics Investigated in the Leuven Growth Study of Flemish Girls

I. *Body size*
- Body Mass:
  - Body weight
- Skeletal size:
  - Height
  - Sitting height
  - Acromial height
  - Trunk height
  - Biacromial diameter
  - Bicristal diameter
  - Chest width
- Bone length of limbs:
  - Forearm length
  - Leg length
- Bone width of limbs:
  - Humerus diameter
  - Femur diameter
- Muscle width:
  - Upper arm circumference flexed
  - Upper arm circumference
  - Forearm circumference
  - Thigh circumference
  - Calf circumference
- Subcutaneous fat:
  - Triceps skinfold
  - Biceps skinfold
  - Subscapular skinfold
  - Suprailiac skinfold
  - Calf skinfold
- Head dimensions:
  - Head circumference
  - Head length
  - Head width

II. *Somatotype*
- Somatotype photograph in three positions:
  - Sheldon trunk index technique (1969)
  - Heath-Carter technique (1975)

III. *Maturity*
- Menarche:
  - Status quo and retrospective method
- X-ray:
  - Tanner-Whitehouse II method (1975)

the representativeness of the sample. The X-rays also make it possible to take anthropometric measurements of the hand. These somatic characteristics with their measurements are summarized in Table 1.7.

Cardiorespiratory Parameters

Considering the selection of the step test in the boys' study and the results of factor analytic studies on cardiorespiratory endurance tests (Van Gerven & Vanden Eynde, 1978), three types of tests were selected. An endurance run consisting of a 480-m shuttle run was chosen as a valid indoor test. A pulse recovery test, known as the one-minute step test, was also retained. Despite its rather low reliability, it served as comparative material with reference to the endurance test on the boys. A work load test, with a gradually increasing work load as a function of body weight, was administered to a random sample of the total group of subjects at each age level. Van Gerven and Vanden Eynde (1978) demonstrated that the parameters from these three tests can be considered as separate factors.

The step test and the 480-m shuttle run were too difficult for girls in the first three grades of primary school and were only administered from the fourth grade onward. Some of the most commonly used parameters of lung function, such as forced expired volume, forced vital capacity, and peak flow were also included in the testing protocol. Table 1.8 gives an overview of the cardiorespiratory and lung function characteristics used.

Table 1.8 Cardiorespiratory Parameters Examined in the Leuven Growth Study of Flemish Girls

Endurance	
Pulse recovery	one-minute step test (starting from 4th grade)
Working capacity	bicycle ergometer test (three stages of 2 min; gradually increasing) watt/kg body weight (electrically braked Siemens-Elema bicycle)
Lung function	peak flow forced expired volume forced vital capacity
Cardiovascular function	pulse rate at rest, diastolic and systolic blood pressure

Sport Skill and Physical Activity

Due to lack of time, only one ball skill test, the basketball dribble test, could be administered in this study although it has been demonstrated (Pauwels, 1977) that a number of separate factors can be isolated in this area. For the same reasons, no other sports skills could be examined.

Participation in sports, the behavioral component of the physical fitness domain, was studied by means of a questionnaire that was sent to the parents and afterwards checked by an interview with the child. For the youngest girls (1st to 6th grade) a physical activity inventory was administered in order to assess child rearing patterns and family lifestyle, through the Environmental Stimulus

Table 1.9 Sport Skill and Physical Activity Examined in the Leuven Growth Study of Flemish Girls

1. *Sport skill*
   - Ball skill — basketball dribble test
2. *Physical activity*
   - Movement activity inventory: Environmental Stimulus for Physical Activity (ESPA) (1st till 6th grade)
   - Sport participation inventory: Different sports practiced and their organizational context (7th till 12th grade)

for Physical Activity Scale. For the girls in secondary schools, an inventory was made of their active participation in different sports. A summary of sport skill and physical activity items is provided in Table 1.9.

Sociocultural Characteristics and Knowledge of Health

Even in an industrialized country such as Belgium, there is a relationship between the sociocultural milieu of the child and its physical fitness. For this reason, a questionnaire was used to gather information on the sociocultural background of the child and its parents (Renson, 1973). In this questionnaire, several sociocultural variables were investigated (Table 1.10). It was sent to the parents, and the accuracy of the answers was checked during a control interview with each child. The sociocultural determinants used in the Leuven Growth Study of Flemish Girls are listed in Table 1.10. In addition, an inquiry was made concerning the child's knowledge of health.

Table 1.10 Sociocultural Determinants Used in the Leuven Growth Study of Flemish Girls

Educational level of the father
Educational level of the mother
Socioprofessional status of the father
Socioprofessional status of the mother
Urbanizational level
Province
Type of housing
Birth size
Birth order
Brothers (*n* of boys in the family)
Sisters (*n* of girls in the family)
Father's age
Mother's age
Sports participation of the father
Sports participation of the mother
Type of schooling
School body

Chapter 2

The Sample

Bart Vanreusel, Jan Simons, and Gaston P. Beunen

As indicated earlier, the Leuven Growth Study of Flemish Girls was designed to provide information concerning the physical fitness of Flemish schoolgirls from 6 to 18 years of age. More precisely, the aim was to draw up a separate assessment of the present state of Flemish schoolgirls at each age level between 6 and 18 years. In order to meet these objectives, Goldstein (1978) demonstrated that a sample of at least 500 subjects in each category is required to obtain reliable estimates of extreme percentiles. Since the study design distinguished 12 school-grade categories, this would mean a sample of 6,000 subjects. Because of the planned differential studies, a larger sample size was required at each age level in order to obtain a sufficient number of observations in some extreme categories (Beunen et al., 1982).

Therefore, taking into account the number of researchers needed and the limitations of time, organizational capacity, and budget, it was decided to test about 10,000 girls over a period of one school year (9 months). The sample would cover Flanders, the northern Dutch speaking part of Belgium. Since Belgian law requires youngsters to attend school from the age of 6 to 16 and most children remain at school until 17 or 18 years of age, it made sense to collect data in schools. A multistage proportional cluster sampling procedure was chosen, considering the need of an adequate sampling frame. In the first stage, a proportionate stratified sample with schools as the primary sampling cluster was selected. The different strata were selected according to the structure of the Belgian school system and to the geographical distribution of the schools. The following stratification criteria were operationalized:

- school level: primary schools
  secondary schools
- geographical distribution of the schools per province: Antwerpen
  Brabant
  Limburg
  Oost-Vlaanderen
  West-Vlaanderen

- school body: private (i.e., Catholic) schools
  state schools
  community schools

The proportions were calculated by the Service of Statistics and Planning of the Belgian National Secretariat of Education (Van Den Bosch, 1979). This first sampling stage resulted in the selection of 88 schools (Table 2.1). The schools were randomly selected from lists of schools provided by the central administration mentioned above.

The sample contained 43 primary schools and 45 secondary schools. Differences between population and sample proportions were not significant. Additionally, after the first selection was carried out, factors such as the size of school and population density of the location of the school were taken into account. Moreover, for the secondary schools, the proportional representation of technical, vocational or general humanity schools in the sample was checked. A few corrections were made in order to match the required proportions.

In the second stage of the sampling, classes of schoolgirls were selected from the six primary school grades and from the six secondary school grades. Thus, entire classes were used as the smallest sampling unit. An overview of the sample

Table 2.1 Number and Percentage of Schools in the Population and in the Sample

		Primary schools				Secondary schools			
		Population		Sample		Population		Sample	
Province	Schoolbody	*n*	%	*n*	%	*n*	%	*n*	%
Antwerpen	Private (Catholic)	347	13.5	5	11.6	264	18.1	9	20.9
	State	67	2.6	1	2.3	81	5.5	1	2.2
	Community	212	8.2	2	4.7	60	4.2	2	4.3
Brabant	Private (Catholic)	249	9.7	5	11.6	156	10.7	5	11.1
	State	63	2.4	1	2.3	73	5.1	2	4.3
	Community	172	9.0	2	4.7	27	1.8	—	
Limburg	Private (Catholic)	232	9.0	5	11.6	134	9.2	5	11.1
	State	51	2.0	1	2.3	50	3.5	2	4.3
	Community	70	2.7	1	2.3	13	0.8	—	
Oost-Vlaanderen	Private (Catholic)	371	14.4	6	13.9	220	15.1	8	17.7
	State	82	3.3	2	4.7	80	5.5	2	4.3
	Community	151	5.9	2	4.7	28	1.9	—	
West-Vlaanderen	Private (Catholic)	332	12.9	8	18.7	202	13.9	7	15.5
	State	60	2.3	1	2.3	62	4.2	2	4.3
	Community	111	4.4	1	2.3	7	0.5	—	
Totals		2,570	100%	43	100%	1,457	100%	45	100%

Note. Total sample = 88 schools.

is shown in Table 2.2. The observed numbers in each grade fit very well the expected numbers, and the differences are not significant. However, primary school girls are slightly underrepresented, whereas secondary school girls are slightly overrepresented. Nevertheless, every grade has a sufficiently large sample.

The total sample consisted of 9,954 girls, 47.6% at primary school level and 52.4% at secondary school level. After this second sampling stage was carried out, the geographical distribution of the subjects was controlled, as presented in Table 2.3. A maximum difference of 1.6% was observed between the proportions in the population and the proportions of the sample. The differences were not significant. Therefore, no corrections were made. The testing, coding, and

Table 2.2 Number and Percentage of Subjects at Each Grade of Primary and Secondary School

	Primary school sample							Secondary school sample					
Grade	1	2	3	4	5	6	Grade	1	2	3	4	5	6
n	754	728	824	763	851	818	*n*	797	893	1,018	795	944	769
%	7.6	7.3	8.2	7.7	8.5	8.2	%	8.0	9.0	10.2	8.0	9.4	7.8
	n = 4,738							*n* = 5,216					
	47.6%							52.4 %					
							TOTAL *n* = 9,954						
							100%						

Note. Expected *n* = 829 for each grade; % 8.3 for each grade.

Table 2.3 Number and Percentage of Girls in the Population and in the Sample in the Five Flemish Provinces

	Total population of schoolgirls		Sample	
Province	*n*	%	*n*	%
Antwerpen	135,424	27.9	2,655	28.5
Brabant	75,018	15.5	1,309	13.9
Limburg	69,490	14.3	1,498	15.9
Oost-Vlaanderen	112,388	23.2	2,030	21.6
West-Vlaanderen	92,661	19.1	1,905	20.2
Other			17	0.2
Total	484,981	100	9,414	100

computing procedures together with the data processing caused a dropout of 256 subjects. Consequently, a final sample size of 9,698 girls remained available for further analysis.

Chapter 3

The Testing Procedure

Renée Colla and Chris Schueremans

In 1979-1980 about 10,000 girls from 6 to 18 years of age from 88 different schools were tested by a team of female investigators. The team consisted of two test coordinators who were responsible for the daily management, one secretary, and twelve test instructors. During one month before starting the project, the team was trained in the administration of the tests. During the testing period, physical education students who had been trained in administering the tests during a course of practical exercises in kinanthropometry assisted the team. Thus, each student participated in a whole week of field work and was responsible for conducting one particular test.

The sample consisted of 88 schools. Each school was given a code number and a separate file in which all the data was stored. A provisional schedule was made with the dates planned for visiting each school. The secretary contacted the different schools by telephone and arranged an interview with the school management. The schools were visited by a research assistant who explained the aims of the project and its procedure in order to ensure a fruitful collaboration.

Each school had to be visited twice, if possible with a one-week interval, by two different research teams. The anthropometric measurements and physiological tests together with the 480-m shuttle run and the control interviews for the social questionnaire took place during the first session. A second session followed one week later. Then the motor tests, the questionnaire on eating habits and hygiene, the spirometry, the X-ray photograph of the left hand, and the ball skill test were administered. During this second session the 480-m shuttle run was repeated and the control interviews for the social questionnaire were completed.

An appointment was made with each school, and a random selection was made of the number of classes to be tested, according to the preset stratified sample distribution. The physical conditions such as temperature and size of the testing room, the power points, infrastructure available, and so forth were checked. All this data was collected on a checklist, on which was also indicated the name of the head and her or his assistant, the best route to reach the school, and the easiest access to the premises and to the testing room. A name list with the birthdays of the subjects to be tested was established or—if not available at that time—was sent to the secretariat in Leuven. All this data was added to the school's file. The social questionnaires were handed out to the pupils by their class tutor. They were filled in at home by the parents and collected before the investigation started in the school.

A personal data form was prepared for each student, featuring the family name, first name, municipality, initials, and the date of the motor test. The birthday and initials were repeated on each page of the data form in order to locate each of the subjects easily by these personal codes. The code on the second page was written in big black letters and was used to identify the three somatotype photographs of each subject. Furthermore, all items were listed on the test form, together with the necessary boxes for registering the results. The test forms for the primary and secondary schools, which were somewhat different, each had a specific color. Each individual test form also had control boxes for indicating the administration of the X-ray and the social and hygiene questionnaire because these items had no direct results. The testing team had two vans for the transport of people and instruments. For the motor test battery, a compact and handy multitest device was designed so that these tests could take place on the minimum surface and in standardized conditions.

The Test Administration

The first session comprised anthropometry, somatotyping, exercise physiology, the endurance test, and the social questionnaire. On the arrival of the test team, the first class was called in and the social questionnaires were collected. In the meantime the members of the testing team installed their instruments in a systematic order so that the subjects were obliged to follow a preconceived circuit. As soon as the pupils arrived, they sat down and listened to the test team leaders who informed them about the aims of the tests and the importance of full cooperation. Each pupil received her individual form and checked the exact spelling of her name and birthday so possible mistakes were corrected. All the test forms of each class were alphabetically ordered. Each fourth test form was marked by a cross in the top corner. The subjects with the marked forms had to perform the ergometer bicycle test instead of the step test.

After this briefing the girls selected bikinis, which were handed out in different sizes, they changed clothes and started the circuit. To facilitate anthropometric measurements, the acromion, the middle of the upper arm, the distal end of the forearm, and the largest circumference of the calf, all taken on the left side of the body, were indicated by a dermographic pencil. The measurements were always done in exactly the same order to avoid missing data. Two persons were used for each test or set of measurements; the responsible test instructor was always the same. The results were read from the instrument, figure by figure, to one decimal point (e.g., body weight: zero, five, three, eight = 053.8 kg). Each figure was repeated and noted down by the second test leader in order to avoid dictation and clerical errors.

Each day four girls, two in the morning and two in the afternoon, were measured for a second time. They received a separate new form marked with the code "control" written in big black letters over the whole page.

After these anthropometric measurements, the girls dressed in their gym suits for a 480-m distance shuttle run, run on the school's playground. One specific test leader checked the accuracy of the questionnaire through a personal control interview with each subject. She managed to interview half of the class during one session. At the end of the interview each girl received an information brochure about the study. These brochures were adapted to the girls' age group: A separate version was developed for primary schools and for secondary schools.

Generally about 25 students completed the circuit within 50 minutes. Having passed all stations of the circuit, the girls dressed again and returned to the classroom. The class teachers were able to attend the whole testing sequence if they wanted to. Most primary school teachers did so. Secondary school students were less keen on the presence of their teacher during the investigation.

During the second visit, the test session consisted of the questionnaire on hygiene and eating habits, the spirometry, an X-ray photograph of the hand, the motor tests, and the ball skill test. The 480-m shuttle run was repeated and the other half of the social questionnaires were checked. During the briefing, the tests were outlined and the questionnaire on hygiene and eating habits was filled in. Then the students put on their gym suits and started the circuit barefooted and without warming up.

One test leader was responsible for each specific test. An important factor of standardization for all the motor tests and also for the 480-m shuttle run was the maximal encouragement of each subject to perform as best she could. The same sequence of the different test stations in the circuit was strictly observed. The test order was established in such a way that the foregoing test would have no negative effect on the following one. The sequence was always the following: (1) flamingo balance, (2) plate tapping, (3) sit and reach, (4) vertical jump or standing broad jump, (5) arm pull, (6) leg lifts or sit-ups, (7) bent arm hang, (8) 50-m shuttle run.

The circuit ended again with the 480-m shuttle run and with the control interview of the social questionnaire of the remaining subjects. During this second session it was also possible to test about 25 students within 50 minutes. Each school was sent a letter of thanks for their collaboration in the project.

Chapter 4

The Description of Tests and Measurements

Albrecht L.M. Claessens, Bart Vanden Eynde, Roland Renson, and Dirk Van Gerven

Description of the Anthropometric Measurements

The measuring techniques described here are based mainly on the procedures given by Cameron (1978, 1984) and Renson, Beunen, Ostyn, Simons, and Van Gerven (1980). In agreement with the recommendations made at the International Congress of 1912 for the unification of anthropometric measurements in Geneva (Duckworth, 1912; Rivet, 1912), and consistent with the measuring procedure followed during the six-year Leuven Growth Study of Belgian Boys (Ostyn et al., 1980), all one-sided measurements were taken on the left side of the body. In order to avoid difficulties with clothing, standardized two-part bathing suits (bikini) were provided to the subjects from the last year in primary school onwards. The test leader provided each girl with a bathing suit of appropriate size after which they undressed in a separate dressing area of the sports hall. Younger girls were measured in their underpants.

Body Weight (WT)

The weight was measured with a beam balance accurate to 0.1 kg. The subject stands straight and is instructed to stand still. In order to select the appropriate weight as quickly as possible, the subject's weight is first measured on a Secca spring balance. (This procedure also provides immediate and permanent control of the calibration of the balance.)

Height (HT)

The height was measured with the Harpenden portable stadiometer (manufactured by Holtain Ltd., Crosswell, Crymmych, Dyfed, Wales). The subject is instructed to stand upright against the stadiometer so that her heels, buttocks, and scapulae are in contact with the backboard and the feet are together. The head should be positioned in the Frankfurt plane, and the headboard of the instrument should be moved down to make contact, with a small pressure, to compress the hair onto the vertex of the skull. With the subject in the correct position she is instructed to stand as erect as possible. The body height is measured to the last completed unit (1 mm).

Sitting Height (SIHT)

Sitting height was measured with the Harpenden sitting height table (manufactured by Holtain Ltd., Crosswell, Crymmych, Dyfed, Wales). The subject is positioned so that the head is in the Frankfurt plane, the shoulders relaxed, the back straight, the upper surface of the thighs horizontal, and the feet supported so that a right angle is formed by the knees. The distance from the seat to the head's highest point (vertex) is then measured and after the headboard is lowered, again with a small pressure to compress the hair, the subject is instructed to sit as straight as possible. The measurement is read to the last completed unit (1 mm).

Leg Length (LELT)

This is the difference between standing height and sitting height.

Acromial Height (ACHT)

Acromial height was measured with an adapted Harpenden portable stadiometer. The subject stands in the same position as for normal height measurement. The free blade of the adapted instrument is moved to the marked lateral tip of the acromial. The measurement is read to the last completed unit (1 mm). Because of the special construction of this instrument a constant of 40.2 mm must be deducted to have the real acromial height.

Trunk Height (TRLT)

This is the difference between acromial height and leg length.

Forearm Length (FALT)

The forearm length was measured with the Harpenden anthropometer (straight blades) (manufactured by Holtain Ltd., Crosswell, Crymmych, Dyfed, Wales). The subject stands relaxed at an angle to the observer so that her left side is turned slightly toward the observer. The counter blade of the anthropometer is applied to the marked head of the radius and the fixed blade to the marked distal end of the radius so that the blade drops into the gap between carpus and radius and is then pushed up against the radius. The measurement is read to the last completed unit (1 mm).

Biacromial Diameter (BADI)

Biacromial diameter is the distance between the tips of the acromial processes. It was measured from the rear of the subject with the Harpenden anthropometer (recurved branches). The position of the lateral tips of the acromial is slightly different in each subject; it is therefore necessary for the observer to carefully mark their exact position before applying the instrument. When the subject stands with relaxed shoulders, the observer applies the anthropometer blades to the lateral tips of the processes. The blades must be pressed firmly against these protuberances so that the layer of tissues that covers them is minimized. The measurement is read to the last completed unit (1 mm).

Chest Width (CHWI)

The measurement was taken with the Harpenden anthropometer, using straight blades. It is the distance between the two most lateral points of the costal cage at the mesosternal level (marked at the level of the third and fourth sternabrae) while the subject stands relaxed with hands on her head. The measurement is taken at the end of a normal exhalation. The general technique is to apply the blades of the anthropometer horizontally to the appropriate landmark. The measurement is read to the last completed unit (1 mm).

Bicristal Diameter (BCDI)

Bicristal diameter is the distance between the most lateral points of the iliac crests, and was measured with the Harpenden anthropometer (straight blades). The subject stands with her front to the observer, in a relaxed position, with the hands away from her sides to ensure a clear view of the iliac crests. The anthropometer is held horizontally and the blades are applied to the most lateral points of the iliac crests. To obtain the 'bony' measurement, the blades must be pressed firmly against the crests so that the layer of tissues that covers them is minimized. The measurement is read to the last completed unit (1 mm).

Humerus Diameter (BEHU)

This is the distance between the two most lateral points of the epicondyli of the humerus and was measured with a spreading caliper accurate to 1 mm (manufactured by Siber Hegner, Zürich). The subject stands relaxed facing the observer with the left arm raised to the level of the shoulder and the elbow bent to a right angle. The caliper is applied to the medial and lateral epicondyles of the humerus with some pressure to compress the soft tissue.

Femur Diameter (BIFE)

This is the distance between the two most lateral points of the epicondyli of the femur and was measured with a spreading caliper accurate to 1 mm. The subject stands facing the observer with her left foot on a small bench so that there is a right angle in the knee. The caliper is applied to the medial and lateral epicondyles of the femur and tightened until the soft tissue is compressed.

Upper Arm Circumference Flexed (UAFC)

The subject stands upright and contracts as far as possible her left m. biceps brachii. A steel tape accurate to 1 mm (Regulator tape, manufactured by Stanley) is passed around the arm so that it touches the skin all round the maximum circumference.

Upper Arm Circumference (UAEC)

The subject stands relaxed, sideways to the observer, with the left arm hanging loose at her side. The steel tape, accurate to 1 mm (Regulator tape, manufactured by Stanley), is passed around the arm at the level of the mid upper arm mark. This landmark is taken as the point on the lateral side of the upper arm midway between the lateral border of the acromial process and the olecranon when the arm is flexed at 90 degrees. The tape is tightened so that it touches the skin all round the circumference but does not compress the tissue to alter the contour of the arm.

Forearm Circumference (FACI)

Maximum forearm circumference is measured at a point immediately distal to the elbow joint. The subject stands relaxed, facing the observer, with her left arm slightly upward and the hand in a supination position. The steel tape (Regulator tape, manufactured by Stanley) is passed around the arm at the maximum horizontal or at the greatest bulge of the muscles. The tape is tightened so that it touches the skin all round the circumference.

Calf Circumference (CACI)

The subject stands erect with her feet slightly apart and her weight evenly distributed on both feet on a bench so that the observer can be near to or at eye level with the calf. The measurement, determined by trial-and-error techniques, is taken horizontally (perpendicular to the long axis) with a steel tape (Regulator tape, manufactured by Stanley) at the maximum circumference of the calf, on the left leg.

Thigh Circumference (THCI)

The subject stands erect with her feet slightly apart and her weight evenly distributed on both feet on a small bench so that the observer can be near to or at eye level with the upper thigh. The steel tape (Regulator tape, manufactured by Stanley) is passed around the left limb just below the gluteal fold and perpendicular to the long axis. The tape is tightened so that it touches the skin all round the circumference but does not compress the tissue to alter the contour of the thigh.

Triceps Skinfold (TRSK)

The triceps skinfold was measured with the Harpenden skinfold caliper (manufactured by British Indicators Ltd., UK) midway between the acromial process and the olecranon (this level is the same as that for the upper arm circumference) on the left arm when relaxed. The subject stands with her back to the observer, and the skinfold is picked up over the posterior surface of m. triceps brachii in a vertical line about 1.0 cm above the marked midpoint. The skinfold caliper, which is held in the right hand with the dial upward, is then applied to the fold just below the index finger and thumb at the marked midpoint of the upper arm. After approximately 3 seconds, the measurement is read to the last completed 0.1 mm.

Biceps Skinfold (BISK)

The biceps skinfold, measured with the Harpenden skinfold caliper, is the exact opposite of the triceps skinfold, being on the anterior aspect of the left arm and at the same midpoint level as described for the triceps skinfold. The subject stands facing the observer, her left arm hanging relaxed with the palm facing forward. The skinfold is picked up in a vertical line about 1.0 cm above the marked midpoint. The caliper is then applied to the fold just below the index finger and thumb at the marked level, and after approximately 3 seconds, the measurement is read to the last completed 0.1 mm.

Suprailiac Skinfold (SISK)

The suprailiac skinfold was measured with the Harpenden skinfold caliper approximately 1 cm above and 2 cm medial to the left anterior superior iliac spine. The subject stands relaxed facing the observer. The skinfold is picked up in a line running parallel to the natural cleavage line of the skin. The caliper then is applied just below the fingers and, after approximately 3 seconds, the measurement is read to the last completed 0.1 mm.

Subscapular Skinfold (SSSK)

The place of measurement, also taken with the Harpenden skinfold caliper, is located immediately below the inferior angle of the left scapula. The subject stands with her back to the observer and her shoulders relaxed with arms hanging loosely at her sides. The skinfold is picked up at an angle laterally and downward, slightly inclined in the natural cleavage line of the skin. The caliper then is applied just below the index finger and thumb and, after approximately 3 seconds, the measurement is read to the last completed 0.1 mm.

Calf Skinfold (CASK)

The skinfold is measured at the level of the maximum calf circumference on the medial aspect of the left calf when the subject is sitting on a bench with a right angle in her knees. The level ought to be marked when the maximum calf circumference is measured. The skinfold is picked up vertically about 1.0 cm above the marked point. The Harpenden skinfold caliper is then applied to the fold just below the index finger and thumb at the marked level. After approximately 3 seconds, the measurement is read to the last completed 0.1 mm.

Sum of Three Skinfolds (SSK3)

This is the sum of the triceps, suprailiac, and subscapular skinfolds.

Sum of Five Skinfolds (SSK5)

This is the sum of the triceps, biceps, suprailiac, subscapular, and calf skinfolds.

Head Circumference (HECI)

The subject sits on a bench (about 40 cm high) sideways to the observer with her head in the Frankfurt plane. The steel tape (Regulator tape, manufactured by Stanley) is passed around the head, over the most anterior part of the head and over the most posterior part of the occiput. Once this is determined, the tape is pulled tight to compress the hair and the measurement is read to the last completed unit (1 mm).

Head Length (HELT)

The subject sits on a bench sideways to the observer with her head in the Frankfurt plane. The length of the head was measured with the Harpenden anthropometer, using recurved branches (manufactured by Holtain Ltd., Crosswell, Crymmych, Dyfed, Wales), from the glabella to the occiput in the midsagittal plane.

Head Width (HEWI)

The subject sits facing the observer with her head in the Frankfurt plane. The width of the head was measured with the Harpenden anthropometer (recurved branches), above and behind the ears in a plane perpendicular to the midsagittal plane.

Description of the Motor Fitness Battery

Most of the test techniques given here have been previously described by Renson et al. (1980) in connection with the Leuven Growth Study of Belgian boys (Ostyn et al., 1980) and afterwards adapted and slightly changed for use in the countries of the Council of Europe (Simons & Renson, 1982). The whole battery was performed by means of a compact ''tubeframe'' constructed in the institute's workshop. For some tests, automated recording techniques were designed. It should also be noted that in the construction of this test battery, special attention has been given to its practical applicability. With the exception of the 480-m shuttle run, only tests have been selected that can be administered in a gymnasium or sports hall (or in any other large room). The test descriptions include the factor measured, the name of the test and its abbreviation, the necessary material, the instructions together with the test-specific directives, and the scoring of the test. First, general testing directives applicable to all of the tests are given. All these directives need careful observation in order to make the testing as objective and standardized as possible.

General Testing Directives

- The subjects performed all motor tests barefooted (except for the 480-m shuttle run) and in sportswear.
- The total testing procedure took place in a large room, gymnasium, or sports hall (a nonslip surface was required for the running and jumping events). The 480-m shuttle run was performed outdoors or in a large hall.
- The test battery was organized in a circuit system with a strict testing order. Each station was therefore marked with its corresponding sequential number.
- The specific directions for each test were carefully observed and were mentioned to each subject in order to make the testing as objective as possible.
- No warm-up or stretching exercises were permitted before the test series.

- The subjects remained inactive between each test.
- The subjects were not allowed to have a previous trial of the test except for those in which it is explicitly stated in the test description.
- The test leader encouraged the subjects to perform the tests as exactly, rapidly or persistently as possible, according to the measured factor.

Flamingo Balance (FBA)

Factor: Body Balance

Material

- An iron beam with a length of 50 cm, 4 cm high and 3 cm wide. (For the first three grades of the primary school a beam of 5 cm breadth was used.) The stability of this beam is ensured by means of two supports 15 cm long and 2 cm wide.
- Stop watch without reset (zero-setting) so that it can be subsequently started and stopped.

Instructions

Try to keep your balance for as long as possible, standing on your preferred foot upon the longitudinal axis of the beam. Bend your other leg backward and grip the back of your foot with your hand on the same side, "standing like a flamingo." Your other arm may be used to keep you well balanced. I will help you to place yourself in the correct position by giving you support on my forearm. From the moment that you release my supporting arm the test will begin. You must try to stay in balance in this position up to a total time of one minute. The test is interrupted and a penalty mark is given each time a loss of balance is registered, namely, when you let go of the gripped foot or when you touch the floor with any part of your body. After each interruption, the same procedure starts over again until the one-minute time lapse is covered.

Directives

- The test leader should place himself or herself before the subject.
- The subject is allowed to have a trial to become familiar with the test and to make sure that the instructions are understood.
- After this trial the test is carried out.
- The stop watch is started when the supporting arm of the test leader is released by the subject.
- The watch is stopped each time that the subject goes out of balance visually by letting go of the gripped foot or when touching the floor with any part of her body.
- After each interruption the test leader helps the subject to place herself in the correct starting position.

Score

- Number of attempts needed to keep in balance on the beam for one minute.
- If the subject reaches 15 interruptions within the first 30 seconds, the test is ended and the subject gets a zero score, which means in fact that the subject is unable to perform the test. This was occasionally observed among the younger, 6 to 9 years age groups.

Plate Tapping (PLT)

Factor: Speed of Limb Movement

Material

- Two plates, each 20 cm in diameter, are horizontally fixed 60 cm apart at the same level on a single support. The plates are set at the level of the hip crest.
- Stop watch.

Instructions

Stand in front of the plates with a slightly spread stance. When I say "ready . . . start!" move the chosen hand back and forth between the two plates as quickly as possible, being sure to touch the plate each time. The test will last 20 sec. Stop at the signal "stop!" One point is scored each time a plate is touched. The test is performed only once.

Directives

- The test leader should stand at the side of the subject.
- In preparation for the test, set the right hand of a right-handed subject on the left plate (left hand of a left-handed subject on the right plate). The test leader must check that the right shoulder of a right-handed subject is positioned roughly in the middle of the two plates (for left-handed subjects the opposite).
- The stop watch is started at the signal "ready . . . start!" and stopped after 20 sec with the signal "stop!"
- It is desirable that an assistant counts the number of taps when an electronic apparatus is not available. In this case, the assistant counts the taps on one plate and doubles this number. The number of incorrect taps is then subtracted from the total. The test leader keeps the time and encourages the subject.
- The subject does not have to tap the plates hard. It is only important to move back and forth quickly.

Score

The score consists of the total number of taps on each of the plates in 20 sec. The score is calculated by multiplying by two the number of correct taps on one plate and by subtracting possible incorrect taps from this total. For instance, 41 x 2 = 82, incorrect touches = 3, and 82 − 3 = a score of 79.

Sit and Reach (SAR)

Factor: Flexibility

Material

- A test table (box) with the following measurements: length 35 cm, width 45 cm, height 32 cm. The measurements of the top plate are length 55 cm, and width 45 cm. This top plate extends 15 cm over the side against which the feet are placed. A scale from 0 to 50 cm is drawn on the top plate.

Instructions

Sit down. Place your feet vertically against the box. Bend your trunk forward as far as possible without bending your knees and with the hands stretched out in front of you. Try to remain still in the farthest position. Use no bouncing movements. The test will be done twice with the best result counting.

Directives

- The test leader stands at the side of the subject and fixes the knees in the extended position.
- The score is determined from the farthest position that the subject can reach on the scale with her fingertips. The subject must hold this position at least for a count of two so that the test leader can correctly read the score.
- When the fingers do not reach an equal position, the average distance of the two fingertips is taken.
- The test must be done slowly and progressively without any bouncing movements.
- The second trial follows after a short rest period.

Score

Only the best result obtained in the two trials counts. The score is given in centimeters reached on the scale on the top of the box. For instance, a subject who can reach to her toes receives a score of 15; one who reaches 7 cm past her toes receives a score of 22.

Vertical Jump (VTJ)

Factor: Explosive Strength

Material

- A blackboard 200 cm high and 60 cm wide is fixed on the wall, with the bottom 155 cm above the ground. The board is divided by horizontal lines placed 5 cm apart. The exact height above the ground is written on the board every 10 cm in order to facilitate reading the results.
- Magnesium chalk.

Instructions

Cover the fingertips of both hands with chalk. Stand in front of the board with both hands stretched above the head. The feet should be together with the heels on the floor. With the body, arms, and fingers completely stretched, make a mark with the fingertips on the board. Now stand sideways, left or right, next to the board. Bend your knees, swing your arms, and jump as high as possible. At the highest point mark the board with the fingertip of the left or right hand. The test is done three times and the best result is taken.

Directives

a. Reaching height

- The test leader stands behind the subject and helps her assume the correct position.

- Check that the heels are on the ground and that the entire body is stretched.
- The reaching height is registered in cm and is measured only once.
- Results that fall between the lines are estimated (with the eye) to the nearest centimeter.
- If the reach of the fingertips of both hands is not equal, ask the subject to make it so. If this is not possible then take the mean height of the two hands.

b. Jumping height

- Depending on whether the subject is right- or left-handed, she takes her place with her right or left side facing the board.
- Emphasis should be placed on bending the knees, swinging the arms, completely stretching the body, and marking the board at the highest point.
- No steps may be taken before the jump.
- During the jump take a position far enough away from the subject and check exactly where the board is touched.
- Each subject has three attempts, and the best effort, written in centimeters, is taken as the score.
- The results that fall between the lines are also estimated to the nearest centimeter by the naked eye.
- The chalk marks on the board should be regularly erased.

Score

The score consists of the difference between the reaching height and the best of the three vertical jumps. For instance, a vertical jump of 270 cm − a reaching height of 224 cm = score 46.

Standing Broad Jump (SBJ)

Factor: Explosive Strength

Material

- A nonslip surface of two judo mats set lengthwise next to each other.
- Horizontal lines are drawn 10 cm apart on the landing mat, parallel to the take-off line.
- A tape measure can be put perpendicular to these lines in order to get an accurate measurement.

Instructions

Stand behind the take-off line with your feet together (barefooted), toes just behind the line. Bend your knees and swing both arms backward. Push off vigorously and jump as far as possible, simultaneously swinging your arms forward. Land with your feet together and avoid overbalancing backward. The test is done twice and the best score is counted.

Directives

- The test leader stands to the side and records the jump distances for the two attempts.

- This jumped distance is measured from the starting line to the rearmost point of contact of the heels. If the position of the heels differs, the distance between the take-off line and the nearest heel is taken as the score.
- If the subject should happen to overbalance backward and touch the floor with some part of the body, a fresh attempt should be allowed.

Score

The best result from the two attempts is taken as the score. The result is given in centimeters. For instance, a subject who jumps 1 m 56 cm receives a score of 156.

Arm Pull (ARP)

Factor: Static Strength

Material

A calibrated dynamometer is fixed to a vertical support. A handle is connected to the dynamometer through a chain via a pulley system. Both the height and the length of the pulling device are adjustable. The chain is fixed at shoulder height, and the length of the cable is adjusted so that the handle is positioned in the plane of the elbow pit of the supporting arm. An indicator needle on the scale of the dynamometer indicates the maximum result. Two supporting grips are provided, one for the right hand and one for the left.

Instructions

Stand sideways with the feet spread. While you support yourself against one of the grips with a horizontally stretched arm, take the handle with the other (the strongest). Pull as hard as possible, as if you were bending a bow. Do not jerk the chain.

Directives

- The test leader places herself or himself in front of the subject and adjusts the chain so that the handle lies in the plane of the elbow pit of the supporting arm.
- The subject should not only pull with the arm muscles but, more important, with the back muscles as well.
- Check that the subject takes a steady position with feet spread.
- Before the test is taken, the test leader must make sure that the dynamometer is set at zero and that the handle is well fixed.
- After a short rest a second attempt is made.
- The indicator needle is not returned to zero after the first attempt, so the test leader has only to check if the second attempt is better than the first.

Score

The best result from the two attempts is taken as the score. The result is read to the nearest 0.5 kg. For instance, a result of 35.5 kg gives a score of 355.

Leg Lifts (LEL)

Factor: Trunk Strength

Material

- Two mats (set lengthwise next to each other).
- Stop watch.
- Assistant.

Instructions

Lie down on your back on the mat with the legs extended and the hands under the neck. First lift both legs up to 90 degrees until they touch my hand. This is the correct position. Let the legs back down. When I say ''start'' lift your two stretched legs up as quickly as possible until they touch my hand. Do this as many times as possible in 20 sec. The legs must return each time to the floor. The legs must remain stretched. Try to keep the pelvis on the ground. Continue these movements as quickly as possible till I say ''stop!''

Directives

- The test leader kneels next to the subject and holds her left hand above the pelvis of the subject so that when the legs are lifted until they touch the hand, they will form an angle of 90 degrees with the trunk.
- The test leader holds her hand at about the height of the knee of the subject.
- The back and shoulders must remain on the ground during the entire test. The help of an assistant is necessary here. With the help of her body weight she can fix the upper arms of the subject to the floor.
- The test leader counts aloud each time that the legs of the subject touch the mat. A complete movement thus includes lifting the legs, touching the hand, and returning the legs to the mat.
- After the instructions are given and before the test begins, the subject should execute the entire movement one time slowly while the test leader reminds her: (a) to lift her legs completely until they touch the test leader's hand, (b) to return her legs each time to the mat, and (c) to keep her legs extended at all times.
- The watch is started at the signal ''ready . . . start!'' and the test begins.
- The watch is stopped after 20 sec.
- The test leader should continually give the correct count aloud.
- Incorrect movements are not counted.
- The test leader must check and see that the legs are lifted to 90 degrees. It may be necessary to move her hand during the test if the position of the subject changes. These shifting movements must be limited as much as possible by the assistant who is pressing on the upper arms of the subject.
- The pelvis may be slightly raised above the floor to allow a correct movement.

Score

The total number of times that the correct movement is completed in 20 sec is taken as the score, for instance, 16.

Sit-Ups (SUP)

Factor: Trunk Strength

Material

- Two mats (set lengthwise next to each other).
- Stop watch.
- Assistant.

Instructions

Lie down on your back on the mat with your hands under the neck, your knees bent (90 degrees), and your heels in contact with the mat. Your elbows must come forward as you curl up, finally touching your knees. You may try one sit-up before the beginning of the test. Be sure that your clasped hands are kept to the back of your neck during the movement. The return to your starting position must be just long enough for your shoulders to touch the mat. When I say "ready . . . start!" you will repeat this action as rapidly as you can during 30 sec. Continue these movements until I say "stop!" You only have to perform this test once.

Directives

- The test leader kneels at the side of the subject, controlling the correct starting position.
- The ankles of the subjects are held by an assistant. With the help of body weight the assistant holds the heels on the mat at all times.
- After the instructions are given and before the test begins, the subject should execute the entire movement one time, to make sure that she has understood the instructions.
- The stop watch is started at the signal "ready . . . start !" and is stopped after 30 sec.
- The test leader counts aloud each time a complete, correct sit-up is performed. One complete sit-up includes curling the trunk up to a sitting position, touching elbows to the knees, and returning the shoulders to the mat. Thus, the counting takes place when the shoulders touch the mat. No counting means that the sit-up was not correctly performed.
- During the performance the test leader corrects the subject if she does not touch the knees with her elbows or does not touch the mat with her shoulders when returning to her starting position.

Score

The total number of correctly performed and fully completed sit-ups within the 30-sec limit is taken as the score, for instance, 15.

Bent Arm Hang (BAH)

Factor: Trunk Strength

Material

- A horizontal bar with a diameter of 2.5 cm set ± 190 cm above the ground.
- Stop watch.

Instructions

Stand under the bar and place the hands on the bar at shoulder width in a forward grip. Lift yourself up (with the help of the observer) until the chin is above the bar. Stay in this position as long as possible without resting on the chin. The test is finished when the eyes fall below the bar.

Directives

- Let the subject stand under the bar with hands in a forward grip on the bar at shoulder width. Be careful: Most subjects place the hands too far apart.
- The height of the bar can be adjusted to the mean reaching height of the test group.
- With the watch ready in the hand, take the subject by the hips and lift her into the correct position.
- The watch is started the moment that the subject's chin is above the bar and the test leader lets her go.
- Swinging movements of the subject should be stopped by the test leader. The test leader encourages the subject.
- The watch is stopped when the subject cannot hold the required position any longer or when the eyes fall below the bar.
- The time is not told to the subject during the test.

Score

The time in tenths of a second is taken as the score. For instance, a time of 17.4 sec = 174, and a time of 1 min 3.5 sec = 635.

Shuttle Run, 50 m (SHR50)

Factor: Running Speed

Material

- Slip-proof 10 m mat.
- Stop watch.
- Measuring tape.
- Chalk or white tape.
- Traffic cones.

Instructions

Get in a ready position behind the line. One foot should be just behind the line. When the starting signal is given, run as quickly as possible to the other line and cross it with both feet. Turn around as quickly as possible and return to the starting line and cross that with both feet. This is one cycle, and it must be completed five times. On the fifth time, do not slow down when coming to the finish but continue running. This test is done once.

Directives

- Two parallel lines are drawn on the mat (chalk or tape) 5 m apart. The mat is 10 m long and 100 cm wide. Apart from the 5-m running zone, two zones of 250 cm behind each line permit the subject to turn around while not leaving the mat.

- The line is 120 cm long, and the ends of each line are marked with cones (indian clubs, blocks, etc.).
- The test leader should make sure that the subject crosses the line with both feet, that she remains in the required path, and that the turns are made as quickly as possible.
- After each cycle the number of cycles completed should be called aloud.
- The watch is stopped when the subject crosses the finish line with one foot.
- The subject must not slip or slide during the test, so a slip-proof standardized mat is necessary.

Score

The time needed to complete the five cycles is taken as the score and written in tenths of a second. For instance, a time of 21.6 sec = 216.

Shuttle Run, 480 m (SHR480)

Factor: Endurance

Material

- Hardened ground, minimum 25 m long (mostly on playground).
- Stop watch.
- Measuring tape.
- Traffic cones.

Instructions

Get in a ready position behind the traffic cone. When the starting signal is given, run to the other traffic cone, run around it, and return to the starting cone. This is one cycle, and it must be completed 12 times.

Directives

- Two traffic cones are placed on the ground 20 m apart.
- The test leader should make sure that the subject is running around the cones.
- After each cycle the number of cycles completed should be called aloud.
- The watch is stopped when the subject crosses the finishing line (= the starting cone).

Score

The time needed to complete the 12 cycles is taken as the score and written in seconds.

Description of the Physiologic Parameters

Spirometry

Factor: Lung Function

Material

- Digital spirometer (Spirotron, Dräger).

- Disposable mouthpieces.
- Nose clip.
- Calibration: The spirotron (Dräger) was regularly calibrated by means of a calibration pump.

Instructions
- Put the nose clip on your nose, breathe as much air as possible into your lungs. Take the mouthpiece into your mouth and, as quickly and completely as possible, exhale all the air through the mouthpiece.

Directives
- The subject stands in an upright position.

Score

(automatically provided by pushing a button on the spirometer)

- Peak flow (L/sec) (PEFL).
- Forced vital capacity (L/min) (FVCA).
- Forced expiratory volume after 0.5 sec in percent of FVCL (FEV 5%).
- Forced expiratory volume after 1 sec in percent of FVCL (FEV 1%).
- Forced expiratory volume after 3 sec in percent of FVCL (FEV 3%).
- Forced expiratory volume in L/min after 0.5 sec (FEV 5S).
- Forced expiratory volume in L/min after 1 sec (FEV 1S).
- Forced expiratory volume in L/min after 3 sec (FEV 3S).

Step Test

Factor: Cardiorespiratory Recovery

Material
- A stable bench 40 cm high.
- A clock-chronometer.

Instructions
- Step on and off the bench once. (If necessary the test leader corrects the individual.)
- Now you will step on and off the bench during 1 minute at the rhythm I will indicate.
- (Immediately after the test) Sit down on the bench.

Directives
- The subjects perform the test barefooted.
- Subjects have to put their whole foot on the bench and not just a part of it.
- The test leader starts the chrono at the onset of the step test and syncopates the rhythm of 4 beats per 2 sec for one cycle.
- The test is administered during the anthropometric session when the subjects have not performed any previous heavy activity.
- The test leader does not allow the subject to stand up during recovery until the end of the pulse rate registration.

Score

- Resting pulse (PRRES): The pulse rate is taken during 30 sec with the subject sitting on the step bench, and is expressed in beats per minute.
- Pulse rate immediately after exercise (PO0): The pulse rate is taken while the subject is sitting on the bench from 5 sec until 35 sec after the completion of the test. The pulse is recorded in beats per minute. The result thus must be multiplied by two.
- Pulse rate one minute after the exercise (PO1): The pulse rate is taken from 1 min to 1 min and 30 sec after the step test. The result is recorded in beats per minute.
- Pulse rate two minutes after the exercise (PRREC): The pulse rate is taken from 2 min to 2 min and 30 sec after the step test. The result is recorded in beats per minute.

Bicycle Ergometer Test

Factor: Cardiorespiratory Resistance

Material

- An electromagnetically braked bicycle ergometer (type Siemens Elema, 380 B).
- A chronometer.
- A cardiotachometer and thermal paper-writer.
- Three precordially fixed electrodes, attachment rings, electrode cream (Siemens).
- Calibration: Regularly the bicycle ergometer was calibrated (a) automatically (calibration button) and (b) by a calibration bar.

Instructions

- The subject is asked to sit on the bicycle; the saddle is adjusted to the individual's most comfortable position.
- Three electrodes are precordially fixed on the chest wall (e.g., intercostal six at the right and left side, 10 cm under the nipples and intercostal two at the left side, just beside the sternum).
- Pulse rate at rest, sitting on the bicycle, is taken.
- The individual has to pedal at about 60 turns per minute, beginning at a work load of one times the body weight during two minutes. Without interruption, the load is increased every two minutes proportional to the body weight. During the second step the load increases 2 watts per kg body weight and during the third step 3 watts per kg body weight. Finally the individual is asked to pedal for another three minutes at zero load at 60 turns per minute.

Scores

- The resting pulse rate is measured by the tachocardiograph and registered on thermal paper by a writer (PORE).
- The heart frequency after pedaling at 1 watt per kg body weight during the first and second minute of exercise is registered (PO1W).

- The heart frequency after pedaling at 2 watts per kg body weight during the third and fourth minute of exercise is registered (PO2W).
- The heart frequency after pedaling at 3 watts per kg body weight during the fifth and sixth minute of exercise is registered (PO3W).
- The recovery rate (cycling at zero load with 60 turns per minute) is registered during the first minute after cessation of the test (PO0E).
- The recovery heart rate during the second minute, cycling at zero load is measured (PO1E).
- The recovery heart rate during the third minute, cycling at zero load is measured (PO2E).

Blood Pressure

Factor: Cardio-vascular Function

Material

- An electronic BOSO-TRON (Germany) apparatus was used. The maximal cuff pression and the rate of pression decrease can be changed manually.

Instructions

- Take the left arm of the sitting subject and palpate the arteria brachialis 3 to 5 cm above the elbow junction at the medial side of the biceps tendon. Place the microphone of the cuff carefully on the place where the arteria was most easily palpitable.
- Ask the subject now not to move her extended, but relaxed, left arm.
- Maximal cuff pression is adjusted to 200 mmHg; the (automatic) decrease of the pression is regulated at about 2 sec per 10 mmHg.

Score

- Systolic blood pressure (BDSY) is registered as the pression at first ''beep'' or light signal on the apparatus.
- Diastolic blood pressure (BDDIA) is registered as the cuff pression at the last ''beep'' or light signal on the apparatus.

Somatotype Photographs

All girls were photographed in the three standardized positions (front, side, and back views) according to the procedure described by Dupertuis and Tanner (1950). For standardizing the subjects' clothing on the somatotype photographs, all girls were dressed in a two-piece bathing suit especially provided for this study. The photographs were taken with a Robot camera (Robot-Motor-Recorder C, manufactured by Robot, Düsseldorf), with a Schneider-Kreuznach lens (Tele-Xenor 1:3.8/75) at f/5.6 and with Panatomic X Kodak film (32 ASA). The lens of the camera was placed 7 m from the center point of the turntable, 97 cm above the floor. Behind the pedestal, at 1.5 m, a white screen was set up. An electronic flash (Metz CT 40) was placed 4.5 m from the pedestal to light the subjects. Behind this, three flashes were positioned on the floor, somewhat inclined upward, illuminating the white screen behind the subjects. In order to make photoscopic somatotype ratings as well as trunk index and other photogrammetric measurements, the photographs were enlarged to 1/8 of the subject's height (the actual conversion factor being 8.33) on Brovira speed paper (BN 310 PF; 24 x 30.5 cm) manufactured by Agfa-Gevaert, Belgium.

Skeletal and Sexual Maturation

Skeletal Maturation

To assess skeletal maturity an X-ray of the left hand and wrist of each subject was taken with an X-ray unit Elinax 60 (62 kV; 15 mA) assembled in a portable apparatus designed and constructed according to the recommendations described in Greulich and Pyle's radiographic atlas of skeletal development of the hand and wrist (Greulich & Pyle, 1966, pp. 254-256). For correct positioning of the hand and wrist, the descriptions given by Tanner, Whitehouse, Marshall, Healy, and Goldstein (1978) and Tanner et al. (1983) were followed, so that the head of the third metacarpal was centered just beneath the tube, with a tube film distance of 76 cm. The exposure time varied between 0.8 and 1.0 sec. Osray M3-18×24 cm (Agfa-Gevaert) was used. Skeletal age was estimated according to the TW2 method published by Tanner et al. (1975), and Tanner et al. (1983).

Sexual Maturation

The occurrence of menarche and age at menarche was determined according to the status quo and retrospective methods only from the fourth grade of primary school (9 to 10 years) on. The data were collected by means of a structured questionnaire (see Appendix A) and a personal interview.

Chapter 5

The Sociocultural and Physical Activity Inventories

Roland Renson and Bart Vanreusel

Information concerning the sociocultural background of the girls and their families and the physical activity habits of the girls was collected by means of a structured written questionnaire that was filled in by the parents and later on verified in an interview with each child. Previous analysis on physical fitness of youngsters has revealed that the level of physical fitness and its basic components is differentiated according to the social and cultural situation of the subjects (Renson, 1973; Renson, 1975; Renson et al., 1978; Renson et al., 1980a; Renson et al., 1980b).

In order to investigate this differentiation, and to control for social and cultural background as independent variables in the global study design, a questionnaire was developed to collect information on this aspect. Earlier studies on the reliability and the objectivity of different parts of the questionnaire (Renson, 1973; Vanreusel, 1985) indicated that it is a reliable instrument to evaluate this aspect of physical fitness. The questionnaire contained the following items:

- educational level of the father
- educational level of the mother
- socioprofessional status of the father
- socioprofessional status of the mother
- urbanization level of the dwelling area
- family size (number of children)
- birth order
- sport participation of the father
- sport participation of the mother

The questionnaires were administered to the parents of the girls. The questionnaires were reexamined and information was, if necessary, added during an interview with each girl. The information was coded into quantitative variables and added to the global data set. The breakdown of the variables into different categories is presented, together with the data, in the chapter on the social and cultural characteristics of the subjects.

Movement Activity Inventory

A movement activity inventory was developed to register the physical activities in the daily life of girls from 6 to 12 years old. In the context of the global project, this inventory estimated the amount of physical activity as a potential contributing and differentiating variable of physical fitness. The inventory was part of the sociocultural questionnaire of the primary school group. It included settings and opportunities for informal motor play activities as well as more formal participation in sports. The following items were included:

1. Spatial play stimulus

Access to play areas, indoor and outdoor, and frequency (seldom or never = X1; from time to time = X2; often =X3)

_____ terrace
_____ backyard or garden
_____ at friends' home
_____ street, neighborhood, or square
_____ playground
_____ wood- or grassland
_____ swimming pool

Score: number of play areas X1 or X2 or X3; minimum score = 8; maximum score = 24

2. Material play stimulus

Availability of activity-stimulating equipment such as toys and children's vehicles (not available = X1; available = X2). These 14 items were:

_____ bicycle
_____ roller skates
_____ skate board
_____ go kart
_____ skipping rope
_____ sledge
_____ badminton or tennis racket
_____ swing or climbing rails
_____ sandbox
_____ children's swimming pool
_____ musical instrument
_____ racket game
_____ ice skates
_____ domestic pet

Score: number of items X1, or X2; minimum score = 14; maximum score = 28

3. Transportation stimulus

Indication of the movement autonomy during transportation to and from school or leisure activities:

(1) driven by car
(2) driven by bus, tramway, or motorbike
(3) walking
(4) by bike

Score: 1 to 4

4. Social participation stimulus

Formal membership in youth associations and/or sport clubs. Both the number and type of organizations were taken into account. Sport club membership was given a higher score than other organizations.

(1) never affiliated
(2) past member of youth association(s)
(3) past member of sport club(s)
(4) current member of a youth association
(5) current member of a sport club
(6) current member of several youth associations
(7) current member of several sport clubs
(8) current member of youth association(s) and sport club(s)
Score: 1 to 8.

5. Participation in camps

This was an evaluation of the girls' previous social and sport participation and their autonomy. Both the number and type of camps were taken into account.

(1) never participated
(2) participation in youth camp(s)
(3) participation in specific sport camp(s)
(4) participation both in youth and specific sport camps
Score: 1 to 4

The inventory was filled out by the girls' parents and was later checked and, if necessary, completed during an individual interview with each girl. All the information was coded into quantitative scores. Different items of the inventory were weighed and combined into two partial scores: (a) spatial stimulus for physical activities and (b) material stimulus for physical activity. At the next stage, all items were combined into one global score called Environmental Stimulus for Physical Activity (ESPA). This combined variable presented a global indication of the degree of involvement in physical activities of the girls from 6 to 12 years of age. The ESPA scores ranged from 37 (minimum score) to 124 (maximum score). The scores were divided into six categories: < 48, very low; 48-60, low; 61-73, below average; 74-86, above average; 87-99, high; and > 99, very high.

Consistency of the ESPA Inventory

In order to estimate the reliability of the ESPA inventory a consistency test was carried out on every item by means of a test–retest procedure. Parents of 207 girls were asked to fill out the questionnaire again, two weeks after the first session. By comparing the item scores of both sessions, the consistency of the answers was measured. The percentage of consistency for the five stimulus items is presented in Table 5.1 The percentage indicates the identical scores in test and retest inventories. The percentage of agreement in the assigned scores of the different items fluctuates between 74.9% and 98.1%. After an in-depth consistency analysis of the inventory (De Roover, 1982), it was concluded that the ESPA inventory could be considered as a reliable evaluation tool.

The cumulative frequencies of the test and retest ESPA scores, as presented in Figure 5.1, also indicate a firm relationship between both measurements. A correlation of .82 between both ESPA distributions confirms the consistency. The figure also shows that the shape of the ESPA distribution approaches the normal distribution curve.

Table 5.1 Environmental Stimulus for Physical Activity (ESPA) Questionnaire: Items and Consistency

Questionnaire items (ESPA)	Test–retest consistency
Spatial stimulus (8 items)	Range: 78.4%-97.9%
Material stimulus (14 items)	Range: 74.9%-98.1%
Transportation stimulus (1 item)	91.7%
Social participation (1 item)	86.1%
Participation (in camps) (1 item)	95.1%

Sport Participation Inventory

For the girls from 13 to 18 years of age, a questionnaire was developed to register their participation in sport activities. Active participation in sports is considered a main item in the physical activity pattern of teenagers. Therefore it is included in the global study on physical fitness, both as a controlling and as a differentiating variable in relation to other components of physical fitness. The sport activities of the girls from 13 to 18 years were recorded by a standardized questionnaire via a retrospective approach: Sport activities during the year before the time of the survey were registered. This inventory was adapted from one previously designed for the Leuven Growth Study of Belgian Boys (Renson, 1973). It was part of the sociocultural questionnaire for this age group. Four aspects of sport participation were covered:

- Type of sport activities (volleyball, swimming, gymnastics, etc.)
- Diversity of sport activities (number of different sports practiced)
- Amount of time spent on each activity (registered in hours per week over a 1-year period)
- Organizational context of sport involvement (i.e., in a club, at school, with friends, in the family, alone)

The questionnaire was designed in such a way that it could be filled in in an easy and correct way. It was completed by the girls' parents and cross-checked during a short interview with each girl. The detailed information on the frequency of sport participation was recorded into a global average score of hours of sport practice per week. Four categories of sport participation were distinguished: 0-1 hour/week, > 1-3 hours/week, > 3-6 hours/week, and > 6 hours/week.

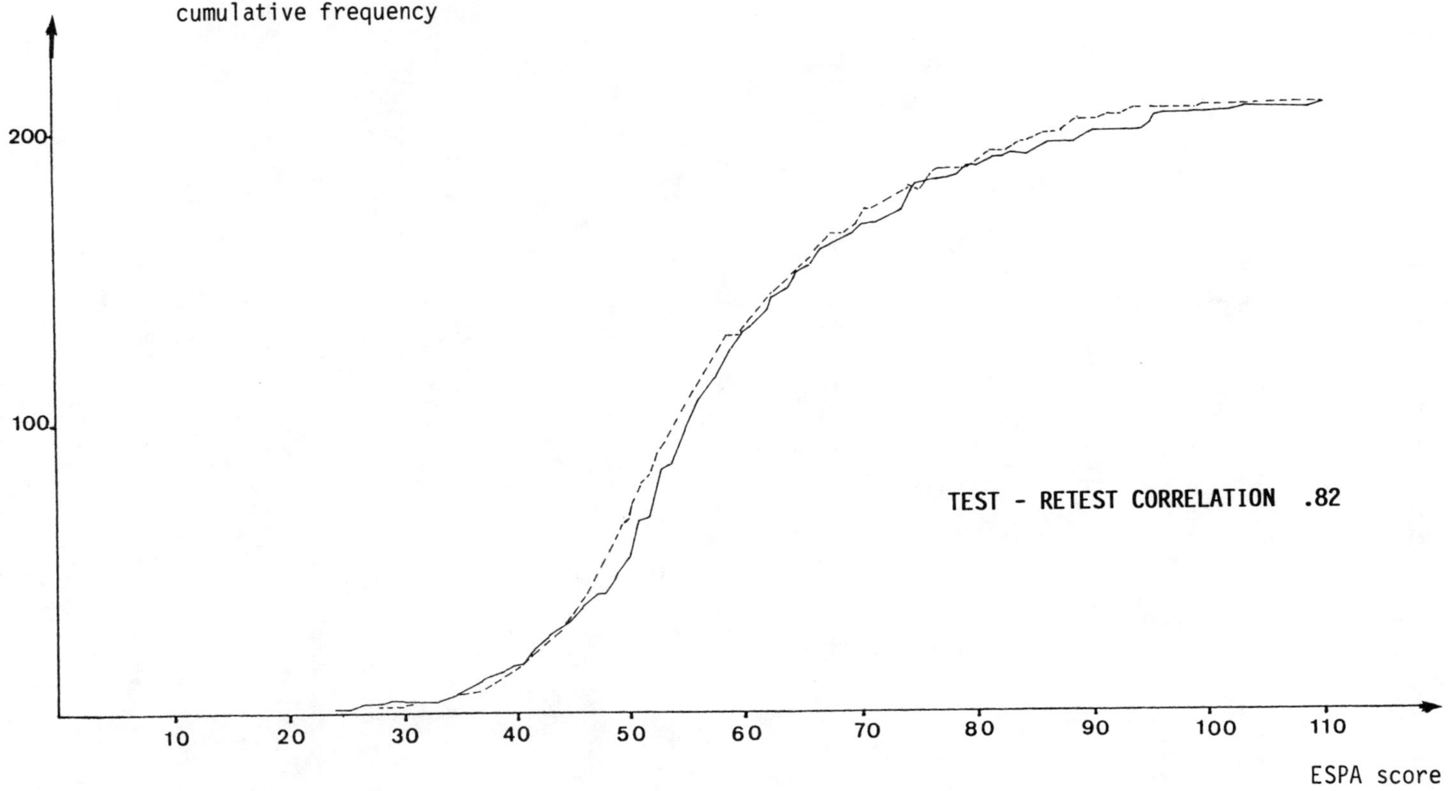

Figure 5.1. ESPA (Environmental Stimulus for Physical Activity of young girls). ESPA score: cumulative frequency curves (N = 207); ——— test, ------------ retest.

Chapter 6

Data Input and Quality Control

Johan A.V. Lefevre, Gaston P. Beunen, and Rita Wellens

In a large epidemiological study, in which an enormous amount of data was collected, a variety of sources of error could endanger the quality of the data. Such errors may arise at the measurement stage by, for example, misreading an instrument, in transcribing data onto forms, in coding answers to questions, or in punching data onto tape or disk. For this reason care was taken to evaluate these errors and, where possible, to limit them, not only during the data collection period but also during the period when data was prepared for entering into the computer and during the data input phase.

Data Collection

All data relating to each girl was recorded on an individual form. Before visiting the schools, the name, birthdate, testing date, school, and subject identification number were recorded on these forms. Most of the test data was directly registered on these forms during the testing sessions. However, there were a few exceptions:

Somatotyping: The Heath–Carter (Carter, 1975) somatotype method was calculated from the measurements. Furthermore, the photographs had to be developed to measure the trunk index (Sheldon et al., 1969), and a new method for girls and women had to be further developed.

Skeletal age: After the X-rays were developed, the skeletal age of each subject had to be assessed according to the Tanner–Whitehouse II method (Tanner et al., 1975; Tanner et al., 1983).

Written enquiries: The answers to the different questions concerning play activities and facilities, sports participation, hygiene, and sociocultural determinants had to be classified into categories and had to be coded in order to obtain quantitative data. A number of indices and derived measurements, such as fat-corrected arm circumference and physical working capacity, were also calculated from the raw data.

Training the Test Instructors

The testing team for the project consisted of 13 females: 2 coordinators, 1 secretary, and 10 test instructors. The team members were instructed in the measuring techniques by experienced kinanthropometrists who were also staff members of the Leuven Growth Study of Belgian Boys (Ostyn et al., 1980). At the beginning of the training period each team member was familiarized with all tests and measurements. Thereafter, each member was trained for a specific task for each of the two testing visits. Throughout the whole testing period each test instructor was responsible for the same task. The instructors were also trained in a second task for which they would be responsible in the absence of the team member in charge of that task. During the 45-day training period, each instructor measured

Table 6.1 Mean Differences, Coefficient of Variation (V), and Correlation Coefficient (*r*) between Independent Measurements by Different Anthropometrists (*N* = 19, 8 to 9-Year-Old Girls)

Measurements	Mean difference	V[a]	*r*
Body weight (kg)	.13	0.5	1.00
Height (cm)	.23	0.3	.99
Sitting height (cm)	.43	1.0	.95
Acromial height (cm)	.10	0.8	.95
Biacromial diameter (cm)	.37	2.0	.92
Bicristal diameter (cm)	.29	1.6	.95
Chest width (cm)	.38	2.6	.90
Forearm length (cm)	.30	1.8	.92
Humerus diameter (cm)	.01	2.0	.88
Femur diameter (cm)	.10	2.2	.84
Upper arm circumf. flexed (cm)	.33	2.6	.96
Upper arm circumf. (cm)	.91	3.6	.97
Forearm circumf. (cm)	.53	1.8	.98
Thigh circumf. (cm)	.77	2.2	.96
Calf circumf. (cm)	.06	0.6	.97
Triceps skinfold (mm)	.12	6.3	.95
Biceps skinfold (mm)	.76	19.1	.88
Subscapular skinfold (mm)	.36	8.3	.98
Suprailiac skinfold (mm)	.95	21.5	.97
Calf skinfold (mm)	.25	5.2	.98
Head circumference (cm)	.14	0.4	.96
Head width (cm)	.09	0.9	.90
Head length (cm)	.07	1.4	.90

[a]Coefficient of variation is a measure of relative error by expressing the technical error relative to the approximate mean $V = \frac{Te}{\bar{X}_t} \times 100$. The technical error of measurement is defined as $Te = \sqrt{\Sigma d^2/2n}$.

or tested about 450 subjects of both sexes and various age groups. After this period inter-observer reliability for the anthropometric measurements was verified between the two instructors and a criterion measurer and between the instructors themselves. One class of third graders was measured by a criterion anthropometrist and by the two trained anthropometrists during one test session. The results of this inter-observer reliability study are summarized in Table 6.1.

The largest inter-examiner differences occur for the skinfolds. However, the mean difference as well as the technical error of measurement and coefficient of variation after this training period are all smaller than those reported for the National Health Examination Survey in the United States (Johnston, Hamill, & Lemeshow, 1972: pp. 57-58; Johnston, Hamill, & Lemeshow, 1974: pp. 65-66), which are of the same magnitude as those reported by other authors (Lohman, 1981). Considering the small age range (8 to 9 years) of the girls under examination it was concluded that the anthropometrists were sufficiently trained to start the main study.

In-Field Reliability

Since the measurement error for the anthropometric measurements could be fairly large, especially during such an intensive testing program, this error was estimated by examining the intra-observer reliability during the course of the study. During the whole study about 100 subjects were measured each day and about 3% of them were re-examined during the same day by the same test instructor. Since the subjects were randomly selected neither the subject nor the anthropometrists were aware of this re-examination at the first measurement. The results of the intra-observer reliability study for 208 girls measured during the whole study are given in Table 6.2.

The indices of relative and absolute measurement error indicate that the measurements were taken with considerable care. The coefficients of variation, as an expression of the magnitude of the measurement error in function of the mean, are small. For lengths, arm circumferences, and head dimensions this coefficient is smaller than 1%. For all other dimensions except skinfolds the variation coefficient varies between 1% and 2%, and for skinfolds it amounts to from 5% to 10%. All these coefficients are lower than those reported by Johnston et al. (1972, 1974). Furthermore, the measurement error for skinfolds is also smaller than that reported by Lohman (1981). It thus seems that the anthropometric dimensions collected in this project are highly reliable. Since all anthropometric dimensions were taken by the same two anthropometrists they gradually became extremely experienced. This certainly contributed to the quality of the measurements. For the performance tests the above procedure could not be followed. Information about the test–retest reliability for 12- to 19-year-old girls, using exactly the same testing procedures, was already available. A summary of the mean correlation coefficients is given in Table 6.3 (for more details see also chapter 1 on the pilot study).

For the 6- to 13-year-old girls a separate test–retest reliability study was set up again using the same testing procedures. In this study 283 girls from two primary schools were tested twice within a one-week interval by the same testing team that conducted the main study.

Table 6.2 Mean Differences, Error of Measurement, Coefficient of Variation, and Correlation Coefficient Between Independent Measurements by the Same Examiner (*N* = 208, 6 to 18-Year-Old Girls)

Measurements	Mean difference	Error of measurement[a]	CV[b]	Correlation
Body weight (kg)	.04	0.41	1.02	1.00
Height (cm)	.18	0.52	0.36	1.00
Sitting height (cm)	.09	0.26	0.34	1.00
Acromial height (cm)	.18	0.46	0.29	1.00
Biacromial diameter (cm)	.02	0.35	1.12	.99
Bicristal diameter (cm)	.01	0.33	1.43	.99
Chest width (cm)	.04	0.37	1.69	.98
Forearm length (cm)	.02	0.25	1.23	.99
Humerus diameter (cm)	.00	0.10	1.80	.96
Femur diameter (cm)	.01	0.09	1.34	.98
Upper arm circumf. flexed (cm)	.02	0.10	0.44	1.00
Upper arm circumf. (cm)	.04	0.10	0.47	1.00
Forearm circumf. (cm)	.02	0.23	1.14	.99
Thigh circumf. (cm)	.20	0.71	1.57	.99
Calf circumf. (cm)	.20	0.56	1.90	.98
Triceps skinfold (mm)	.21	0.71	5.44	.98
Biceps skinfold (mm)	.06	0.44	6.56	.97
Subscapular skinfold (mm)	.10	0.94	10.54	.96
Suprailiac skinfold (mm)	.14	0.77	8.05	.98
Calf skinfold (mm)	.15	0.86	6.25	.98
Head circumference (cm)	.03	0.19	0.36	.99
Head width (cm)	.00	0.09	0.64	.97
Head length (cm)	.02	0.12	0.67	.97

[a]Error of measurement $= \frac{S\sqrt{1 - r^2}}{\sqrt{2}}$ where S is the pooled standard deviation of the two sets of measurements and r is the correlation between measurements.

[b]CV $= \frac{(100 \times \text{error})}{\bar{X}}$

In general, the reliability coefficients found for primary school girls (Table 6.4) were of the same magnitude as for the secondary school girls (Table 6.3). Fairly good reproducibility was found for most motor ability items, with the exception of leg lifts, plate tapping, and 480-m shuttle run. The lung function parameters are reasonably reliable except in the youngest age groups for which low coefficients were observed. The significant difference between the means for several tests indicates a testing effect. All retest results were better than the test results.

Table 6.3 Mean Test–Retest Reliability Coefficients of Motor Abilities and Cardiorespiratory Characteristics for 11- to 19-Year-Old Girls

Test	Mean *r*
Motor abilities (377 girls, 11-19 years)	
Arm pull	.85
Bent arm hang	.87
Vertical jump	.78
Standing broad jump	.91
Leg lifts	.77
Sit-ups	.84
Shuttle run 50 m	.80
Plate tapping	.79
Sit and reach	.94
Flamingo balance	.83
Bicycle ergometer test (161 girls, 12-19 years)	
Heart rate at rest	.61
Heart rate after 2' 1 Watt/kg	.78
Heart rate after 4' 2 Watt/kg	.76
Heart rate after 6' 3 Watt/kg	.74
One-minute step test (65 girls, 12-13 years)	
Heart rate at rest	.36
Heart rate after 30''	.60
Heart rate after 1'30''	.68
Heart rate after 2'30''	.63

Note. Adapted from Beunen et al., 1977 and Simons et al., 1978.

Quality Control in Variable Construction

Anthropometric dimensions, motor abilities, lung function, and cardiorespiratory characteristics are all recorded on test forms and can be used for statistical treatment or for the construction of derived variables such as anthropometric indices and PWC170 (physical working capacity). Other parts of the data collected need considerable further analysis before they can be subjected to statistical treatment. Also in this part of the study care was taken to guarantee the quality of the collected variables. For skeletal age assessment two estimators were trained and their estimations were compared with those of RHW and NC from the Institute of Child Health in London and with a self-taught assessor (GB). The assessments of this assessor correspond very closely with those of the originators of the Tanner–Whitehouse technique (TWII) (see Beunen & Cameron, 1980).

Table 6.4 Test–Retest Reliability Coefficients for Motor Abilities and Cardiorespiratory Characteristics for 6- to 13-Year-Old Girls (N = 283)

Test	Mean difference	t	Total r	Mean r
Arm pull	1.5 kg	5.6*	.84	.72
Bent arm hang	1.3 sec	4.0*	.80	.81
Vertical jump	0.1 cm	0.2	.98	.96
Standing broad jump	2.1 cm	3.1*	.89	.84
Leg lifts	0.7	3.2*	.61	.60
Sit-ups	0.1	0.9	.82	.80
Shuttle run 50 m	0.4 sec	6.2*	.85	.77
Plate tapping	5.4	14.9*	.87	.68
Sit and reach	0.9 cm	5.3*	.89	.89
Flamingo balance	1.0	3.8*	.80	.70
Shuttle run 480 m	2.2 sec	1.9	.54	.56
Peak flow	0.3 L/sec	5.5*	.84	.71
Forced vital capac.	0.1 L	0.3	.82	.69
Forced exp. vol. 1 sec	0.1 L	1.2	.85	.66
Forced exp. vol. 3 sec	0.1 L	0.6	.84	.64

*$p < .01$.

During the training period about 350 X-rays were estimated. The two estimators assessed a number of X-rays on their own, thereafter together, and then together with the criterion estimator (GB). After this period intra- and inter-reliability was checked within and between the two estimators, and with RHW, NC, and GB. Within the context of this manuscript these results cannot be reported in detail; only the inter-observer agreement with GB is given in Table 6.5. It is clear that very high inter-observer agreement was obtained after the training period; for all bones together an agreement of 89.5% or 92.7% was found. When there was disagreement only a difference of one stage was observed.

After the training period the following procedure was adopted. After 100 estimations, four X-rays were randomly selected and re-estimated by the same assessor, and another four were re-estimated by the second observer. In the beginning after 1,000 X-rays, and thereafter after 1,500 X-rays, the standard set of 113 X-rays of the Institute of Child Health, courteously provided by Professor Dr. J.M. Tanner, was re-estimated. The results of these controls are given in Table 6.6. The intra-observer agreement is somewhat better for the second assessor but is very high for both observers and comparable to that of NC and GB (Beunen & Cameron, 1980). The somewhat lower intra-observer agreement of the first assessor is probably also reflected in the lower inter-observer agreement (84.5% with GB and 82% with RHW) as compared to the results for the second observer (85.9% with GB and 87% with RHW). Here also high inter-observer agreement was found especially between the two assessors themselves (obs. 1–obs. 2 over-

Table 6.5 Inter-Observer Agreement Between the Two Novice Assessors and an Experienced Assessor (GB) After the Training Period

Ossification center	% Agreement observer 1	% Agreement observer 2
Radius	93.3	91.1
Ulna	84.4	93.3
Metacarpal 1	88.9	82.2
Metacarpal 3	82.2	88.9
Metacarpal 5	97.8	95.6
Proximal phalanx 1	88.9	93.3
Proximal phalanx 3	82.2	88.9
Proximal phalanx 5	88.9	86.7
Middle phalanx 3	82.2	91.1
Middle phalanx 5	91.1	95.6
Distal phalanx 1	84.4	91.1
Distal phalanx 3	93.3	95.6
Distal phalanx 5	84.4	93.3
Capitate	100.0	100.0
Hamate	93.3	97.8
Triquetral	88.9	95.6
Lunate	86.7	91.1
Scaphoid	88.9	88.9
Trapezium	100.0	97.8
Trapezoid	91.1	95.6
All bones (20)	89.5	92.7

all agreement of 86.9%). During the whole period the agreements within and between observers remained at about the same level as the mean agreement reported in Table 6.6.

These results indicate that the random assessments of the about 5,000 X-rays carried out by each of the observers are in very good agreement. During 6 months they each estimated about 50 X-rays each day. For the enquiries concerning the sociocultural background of the child's family, the sport participation, and play activities and facilities, codification schema were constructed mainly based on previous experience in the Leuven Growth Study of Belgian Boys (Ostyn et al., 1980). The coding of the questionnaires was carried out by two assessors under the supervision of RR, who coded the more than 20,000 questionnaires in the above-mentioned study. The reliability of this questionnaire was checked both by re-applying the questionnaire after a period of one year and by a separate coding procedure by an independent assessor. From these findings it appeared that the determination of the socioprofessional status shows greater stability than the educational level of the parents (Renson, 1973). The introduction of a control interview with each girl allowed the acquisition of more precise data and the detection of definite answer verifications.

Table 6.6 Intra- and Inter-Observer Agreement Between Independent Assessments by Different Observers

	Intra-observer agreement		Inter-observer agreement				
Ossification center	obs1	obs2	obs1 — obs2	obs1 — GB	obs1 — RHW	obs2 — GB	obs2 — RHW
Radius	89.3	93.8	88.5	82.8	77.2	79.1	82.1
Ulna	86.5	94.2	88.8	76.2	88.2	80.3	84.2
Metacarpal 1	82.1	91.9	77.2	80.6	82.0	80.0	88.6
Metacarpal 3	89.0	90.4	82.5	78.4	79.8	79.4	87.8
Metacarpal 5	83.9	92.8	84.8	79.3	82.2	83.8	85.7
Proximal phalanx 1	88.2	93.6	88.2	83.3	79.7	79.7	87.7
Proximal phalanx 3	88.7	94.3	83.3	84.3	78.3	84.9	86.8
Proximal phalanx 5	87.1	93.5	85.6	85.4	82.9	83.9	89.2
Middle phalanx 3	92.8	95.9	85.4	81.6	77.9	87.3	89.2
Middle phalanx 5	87.8	91.8	86.1	83.7	83.0	83.6	87.4
Distal phalanx 1	87.0	89.6	79.5	83.8	83.0	83.6	84.4
Distal phalanx 3	86.3	89.8	86.6	83.8	70.0	87.7	75.3
Distal phalanx 5	89.0	91.7	85.6	77.7	81.6	83.9	83.9
RUS-bones	87.3	92.5	84.7	81.6	80.6	82.6	85.6
Capitate	93.0	92.5	94.3	92.7	83.4	91.6	87.4
Hamate	85.7	91.9	85.3	83.4	73.1	86.7	85.0
Triquetral	87.8	92.6	91.8	89.8	79.3	89.3	87.4
Lunate	91.4	92.3	93.8	92.8	92.8	93.6	93.5
Scaphoid	94.2	94.4	89.6	89.8	86.2	89.9	90.0
Trapezium	86.0	95.6	92.5	83.2	90.4	84.6	92.0
Trapezoid	92.0	93.7	90.7	91.0	92.6	89.2	91.7
Carpals	90.0	93.2	91.1	90.0	84.5	89.2	89.5
All bones	88.2	92.7	86.9	84.5	82.0	85.9	87.0

Data Input

Magnetic cassette tapes were used as storage medium. By means of a BASIC program, all the raw data of each subject were punched a first time. In the next stage, the raw data were punched a second time to detect and to correct punching errors. Separately for each subject, the data of the first punching were reloaded into the memory of the computer. Subsequently, on the analogy of the first time, the data were punched again, with one exception. After punching each value, this value was compared with the value of the first punching. If the two values were identical, the program continued. If the two values were different, then the computer answered with a beep and with the message that the two values were different. In this case, the value was punched a third time. This procedure was repeated until two independently punched values were identical. Once finished with the second punching, the data, free from punching errors, was transferred to a magnetic cassette tape. The last step was the transmission of the data from the tapes to a direct-access file on the mainframe.

Data Cleaning

If a variate has a well-defined range (e.g., a value 0-9 for the variable urbanization level), a check for illegitimate values is easy. Similarly if the value of one such variate is logically dependent on the value of another, cross-checks can be carried out. With a continuous scale, checks must identify outlying observations or suspicious values worthy of further inspection. To identify such values, it is necessary to set up limits beyond which values must be checked. Therefore a file was created with data ($N = 650$) from all age categories. Experts checked all the data (by means of frequencies and plots) separately for each chronological age interval (N = 50). Once this job had been done, errors were corrected. Subsequently, minimum (P3) and maximum (P97) limits were calculated for four different age groups (< 8.50 years, 8.50 − 12.50 years, 12.50 − 16.50 years, > 16.50 years). All the individual data were compared with the upper and lower limits for the age category in question, and a list with possible outliers was printed. Such outliers were checked and if necessary corrected or otherwise deleted. Important criteria to decide whether a value should be considered as an error were:

1. If an extreme value for a certain variable was accompanied by extreme values of other variables, and if logical communality was found in the nature of these variables and in the direction of the eccentricities, the extreme value was not considered as an error.
2. If an extreme value was not accompanied by extreme values of other variables, the individual score sheet was consulted. An erroneous data value may be thought to fall within the tolerance level of the variable considered, yet may not be acceptable when compared to the same subject's value for other related variables.

Using the data of the cleaned file ($N = 650$), a stepwise regression procedure was carried out for each anthropometric and motor characteristic as dependent variable and the other anthropometric/motor characteristics as independent variables, for six age groups. Only when $R > .80$, was a regression equation formulated with the significant entered predictor variables. This was never the case for the motor characteristics since the different tests measure independent motor dimensions. Twenty-four anthropometric variables conformed to the requirement of $R > .80$. These regression equations were carried out on the data of 250 subjects who were selected at random (250 × 24 = 6,000 predictions). Outliers were defined when the recorded value differed too much from the estimated value; namely, when the difference between the recorded value and the estimated value was greater than 2.58 times the standard error of measurement. Only 18 values exceeded these tolerance limits. This means 0.3% (18/6,000) of what can be expected at random. It was then decided that this procedure did not produce a significant improvement of the quality of the data.

Creation of the SAS File

Once all the detected errors were corrected or deleted, the direct access file was copied as a sequential file. Finally, an SAS file was created for the statistical analyses. The different codes as missing values were all converted to SAS missing values, and the necessary derived variables (151 variables) were calculated using SAS statements.

Chapter 7

The Construction of the Growth Standards

Magda Vuylsteke-Wauters and Johan A.V. Lefevre

To construct the growth standards, the total age range was divided into 25 half-year age categories from 6.0-6.5 years of age to 18.0-18.5 years of age. In each interval, the raw percentiles P3, P5, P10, P25, P50, P75, P90, P95, and P97 were calculated on the bases of 175 up to 483 points. Together, the 25 P50 values form the raw median curve, which was then smoothed according to an approximation of splines. According to Smith (1979) splines can be defined as follows:

> Splines are generally defined to be piecewise polynomials of degree *n* whose function values and first (*n*-1) derivatives agree at the points where they join. The abscissas of these joint points are called knots. The number and degree of the polynomial pieces and the number and position of the knots may vary in different situations.

If the knots are fixed and the degree of the polynomial is known, then ordinary regression can be applied for the fitting of the spline. Cubic splines were used since a fairly smooth curve can be obtained assuming continuity restrictions, and yet they have the power to incorporate several different trends in the data simply by increasing the number of knots. The half-year age points from 6 to 19 years were selected as the possible candidates for the knots. In order to find out the most suitable knots a stepwise regression was applied.

The Algebraic Representation of Splines

By introducing the $^+$ function, the implementation of spline regression is straightforward. The $^+$ function is defined as:

$$\begin{aligned} x^+ &= x \text{ if } x > 0 \\ &= 0 \text{ if } x \leqslant = 0 \end{aligned}$$

As an example we first considered the particular case of a piecewise quadratic spline in x with a knot at t and no smoothing conditions:

$$S(x) = \beta_{00} + \beta_{01}x + \beta_{02}x^2 + \beta_{10} + \beta_{11}(x - t)^+ + \beta_{12}[(x - t)^+]^2 + \epsilon \tag{1}$$

More generally, with k knots, $t_1 < t_2 \ldots < t_k$, and the $(k + 1)$ polynomial pieces each of degree n, we may write a spline model with no continuity restrictions as follows:

$$s(x) = \Sigma\beta_{oj}x^j + \Sigma\Sigma\beta_{ij}[(x - t_i)^+]^j + \epsilon \tag{2}$$

where summation is made for $j = 1, \ldots, n$ and $i = 1, \ldots, k$. It is easy to see that (1) is continuous if $\beta_{10} = 0$. With the same remark $S(x)$ in (2) can be made continuous at a knot t_i by omitting the constant terms:

$$\beta_{i0}[(x - t_i)^+]^0$$

The model that was choosen for fitting the percentile curves is a cubic spline that is continuous at all the knots, so the full regression model can be written as:

$$\begin{aligned} s(x) &= \beta_{00} + \beta_{01}x + \beta_{02}x^2 + \beta_{03}x^3 \\ &+ \beta_{11}(x - t_1)^+ + \beta_{12}[(x - t_1)^+]^2 + \beta_{13}[(x - t_1)^+]^3 \\ &+ \beta_{21}(x - t_2)^+ + \beta_{22}[(x - t_2)^+]^2 + \beta_{23}[(x - t_2)^+]^3 \\ &\quad + \ \ldots \ + \\ &+ \beta_{k1}(x - t_k)^+ + \beta_{k2}[(x - t_k)^+]^k + \beta_{k3}[(x - t_k)^+]^3 + \epsilon \end{aligned} \tag{3}$$

The Stepwise Regression Method for Defining the Knots

Model (3) was estimated by the SAS procedure STEPWISE (SAS Institute, 1982), in which the linear term in x was forced in the model for the linear trend. The other terms in the equation are entered sequentially by the forward selection technique. As a result of this method the estimates of β_{ij} were obtained, which are significantly different from zero. Not only was a spline function with some knots obtained, but also the possibility that the piecewise polynomials fitted between two knots allowed to be of different degree was included.

Once the estimates of the β_{ij} that are significantly different from zero were known, the full regression model was applied to the P50 values using the SAS procedure REG (SAS Institute, 1982). The predicted P50 values were compared with the observed P50-values and residuals were calculated. By means of the one-sample runs test (Siegel & Castellan, 1988), the randomness of the order of the positive and negative residuals was tested. All the tests were not significant. Since the residuals are small and the positive and negative residuals occur at random, we may conclude that the approximation of the raw median curve produces a good fit. The residuals were then subtracted from the other calculated raw percentiles at each age level (P3, P5, P10, P25, P75, P90, P95, and P97).

The last step in the construction of the growth standards was a reiteration of the STEPWISE REGRESSION and REGRESSION procedures on these corrected percentiles. The final results were predicted values for all considered percentiles (25 age intervals). These predicted values were then plotted against age by the SAS/GRAPH procedure GPLOT (SAS Institute, 1985). The different points were joined using the spline interpolation option. This routine uses a piecewise third-degree polynomial for each set of two adjacent points. The polynomial passes through the plotted points and matches the first and second derivatives of neighboring segments at the points. The norm scales and profile charts were then derived from the growth standards.

Chapter 8

Sociocultural Characteristics of the Subjects

Roland Renson and Bart Vanreusel

This chapter provides information about the social and cultural background of the girls in the study. More specifically, the educational, socioprofessional and sport participation status of the parents, the urbanization level of the living area, the family size, and the birth order are presented. The data offer a more detailed insight into the composition of the sample. The data will also be used as independent variables in future analysis of sociocultural differentiation of growth and fitness.

Educational Level of the Parents

Eight different educational levels were identified (Renson, 1973). About 50% of the fathers and about 40% of the mothers of the girls have an educational status beyond primary school level. Only a relative minority of parents have an educational status of college or university level. The number of parents gradually decreases with increasing educational status. The general educational level of the mothers is lower than the educational level of the fathers. Whereas the primary school level is overrepresented among the mothers, among fathers the percentage with a college or university degree is double that of the mothers (see Tables 8.1 and 8.2).

Socioprofessional Status of the Father

The position of the girls in the social and economic structure of society was estimated through the socioprofessional status of their parents according to Cliquet (1963). About 25% of the fathers hold a working class position varying from unskilled to skilled labor. About 5% of the parents occupy a very high socioprofessional position. The category of higher executive and managing functions is strongly represented. A remarkable time trend is shown in the socioprofessional

Table 8.1 Educational Level of the Girls' Fathers (in %)

Educational level	Girls Age 6-12 (n = 4,552)	Girls Age 13-18 (n = 4,506)	Group code Girls Age 6-12	Group code Girls Age 13-18	
Primary school	32.09	37.2	46.4	51.7	primary school
Vocational school	14.4	14.5			
Technical school (lower grade)	13.4	10.7	23.3	18.5	lower secondary school
Secondary school (lower grade)	9.9	7.8			
Technical school (higher grade)	7.1	8.9	15.5	18.0	higher secondary school
Secondary school (higher grade)	8.4	9.2			
Higher nonuniversity	10.5	6.7	14.8	11.8	college & university
University	4.3	5.1			
Total	100	100	100	100	

Table 8.2 Educational Level of the Girls' Mothers (in %)

Educational level	Girls Age 6-12 (n = 4,502)	Girls Age 13-18 (n = 4,549)	Group code: Girls Age 6-12	Group code: Girls Age 13-18	
Primary school	36.9	41.2	57.5	62.1	primary school
Vocational school	20.6	20.9			
Technical school (lower grade)	9.7	9.3	16.1	16.0	lower secondary school
Secondary school (lower grade)	6.4	6.7			
Technical school (higher grade)	9.9	8.9	19.2	16.6	higher secondary school
Secondary school (higher grade)	9.3	7.7			
Higher nonuniversity	6.3	4.6	7.2	5.3	college & university
University	0.9	0.7			
Total	100	100	100	100	

Table 8.3 Socioprofessional Status of the Parents (in %)

	Girls Age 6-12 (n = 4,618)	Girls Age 13-18 (n = 4,535)
Socioprofessional status of the father		
Unskilled laborers	3.4	4.3
Semiskilled laborers	11.2	8.9
Skilled laborers	11.2	10.5
Farmers	7.9	10.4
Merchants & artisans	13.5	13.7
Clerks	4.6	6.4
Lower executive functions	10.5	8.2
Higher executive and managing functions	32.8	32.7
Intellectual and socioeconomic upper class	5.9	4.9
Total	100	100
Socioprofessional status of the mother		
Professionally active	40	27
Housewife	60	73
Total	100	100

Note. The socioprofessional status of the father was categorized according to Cliquet (1963).

position of the mothers. While only 27% of the mothers of the older girls are professionally active, this increases to 40% of the mothers of the younger girls. The mothers of the younger girls are presumably younger, which partially explains this trend (Table 8.3).

Urbanization Level

The urbanization level of the dwelling area (Hoge Raad voor de Statistiek, 1967) can be considered as an important environmental aspect in the lifestyle of the girls studied. About half of the sample lives in a semi-urban environment and about one third comes from an urban area. On the contrary, only a relative minority of the girls live in a rural area. This overrepresentation of urban and semi-urban dwelling areas is typical for the present sociogeographic situation in Flanders. Since its socioeconomic and industrial development is reflected in an increasing degree of urbanization, this in turn is reflected in the composition of the sample (Table 8.4).

Family Size and Birth Order

Six family size categories and six birth order rank categories were distinguished; families with six or more children were grouped into one category (Renson, 1973).

Table 8.4 Urbanization Level of the Dwelling Area (in %)

	Girls Age 6-12 (n = 4,735)		Girls Age 13-18 (n = 4,642)	
Agrarian municipality	6.6		6.2	
Semirural municipality	4.5	14.9	4.1	16.7 rural area
Small rural community	3.8		6.4	
Rural community	25.5		27.1	
Small industrialized center	7.2	52.3	6.5	47.9 semiurban area
Small town	19.6		14.3	
Town	18.0		17.4	
Regional center	7.8	32.8	5.9	35.4 urban area
Urban agglomerations	7.0		12.1	
Total	100	100	100	100

Note. The level of urbanization was coded according to the High Council for Statistics (Hoge Ra voor de Statistiek, 1967).

Table 8.5 Family Size: Number of Children (in %)

	Girls Age 6-12 (n = 4,760)	Girls Age 13-18 (n = 4,640)
One child	14.5	11.1
Two children	37.1	27.9
Three children	24.7	23.9
Four children	12.1	17.9
Five children	6.1	8.7
Six or more children	5.5	10.8
Total	100	100

The two-child family is more frequently represented than any other family size. It is notable that the two-child family accounted for almost 28% among the older girls and for more than 37% among the younger girls. Large families are less frequent among the younger girls. Whereas families of six or more children still account for more than 10% of the older girls' families, this drops to 5.5% among the younger girls' families. As far as the birth order is concerned, the majority of the girls are first- or second-born children, which is obviously caused by the high frequency of two-child families. The higher the birth order of the girls, the smaller the percentage becomes (Table 8.5 and 8.6).

Sport Participation of the Parents

Studies on sport socialization processes of children attribute significant importance to the sport role models of the parents. Four categories were operationalized on the basis of the age period of sport participation (Renson, 1973). Considering the parents as major socializing agents, the girls surveyed were not in a favor-

Table 8.6 Birth Order of the Girls (in %)

	Girls Age 6-12 (n = 4,758)	Girls Age 13-18 (n = 4,637)
Only child, or first born of 2 or more children	41.8	37.6
Second-born child	29.8	28.2
Third-born child	14.7	16.1
Fourth-born child	7.0	8.8
Fifth-born child	3.5	4.4
Sixth- or later-born child	3.2	4.9
Total	100	100

Table 8.7 Sport Participation of the Parents (in %)

	Father		Mother	
	Girls Age 6-12 (n = 4,580)	Girls Age 13-18 (n = 4,548)	Girls Age 6-12 (n = 4,564)	Girls Age 13-18 (n = 4,533)
Never participated	32	32	54	45
Participated before 18 years of age	2	2	2	2
Participated between 18 and 30 years of age	11	14	5	4
Participated after 30 years of age	55	52	39	38
Total	100	100	100	100

able position. Data reveal that more than half of the mothers and about one third of the fathers had never practiced any sport. After the age of 30, however, over 50% of the fathers and almost 40% of the mothers were actively engaged in sport or were still active at the time of the survey (Table 8.7).

Chapter 9

Physical Growth, Maturation, and Performance

Gaston P. Beunen and Jan Simons

Growth, maturation, and physical development are essential in the lives of humans, and differences in these contribute greatly to the variation seen in adults. The characterization of these processes is thus important for a better understanding of human biological variation, for the identification of abnormalities, and for better guidance and counseling of youngsters. In Belgium several multidisciplinary growth studies were conducted in the past but were not focused on the growth, maturation, and physical development of girls aged 6 to 19 years.

Changes in Growth and Performance According to Age

From birth to adulthood, both stature and weight follow a growth pattern characterized by a rapid growth in the first year of life gradually declining until adolescence, rapid gain at adolescence, and slow increase and eventual cessation of growth on the attainment of adult stature (Malina, 1974, 1978, 1986a; Tanner, 1962, 1978). Recently a number of authors have provided evidence for a small mid-growth spurt in height and probably also in other body dimensions (Gasser et al, 1984; Meredith, 1981; Tanner & Cameron, 1980). The general growth curve is not only followed by stature and weight but also by most other external body dimensions such as bone lengths, breadths, circumferences, and specific tissues such as muscle tissue (Malina, 1986a).

Subcutaneous fat at triceps and subscapular sites increases during the first year of life, thereafter it decreases until the age of 7 to 8 years, after which it increases (Cronk & Roche, 1982; Tanner & Whitehouse, 1975). Nor do the dimensions of the brain and head follow the general growth curve. The brain and its constituent parts, the head and upper face, experience rapid growth early in life so that by the age of 7 years the brain and its related structures have attained approximately 95% of their adult size. Furthermore, an adolescent spurt in head circumference is demonstrated (Roche, Mukherjee, & Guo, 1986). Recently

Roche, Mukherjee, Guo, and Moore (1987) also have published reference data for head circumference based on a sample of 888 children.

Before adolescence, small but consistent differences between the sexes are already present, but with the attainment of puberty and the hormonal changes that take place at this period (Guyda, 1986) the differences in size and proportion are accentuated. Girls gradually develop smaller body dimensions than boys in stature, weight, lengths, most circumferences, breadths, and muscle tissue. From 6 years onwards boys have a greater lean body mass than girls. On the average, girls exceed boys in absolute and relative amounts of fat. The differences are not large during childhood, but as adolescence approaches, the differences are magnified and they persist through adolescence. The broadening of the shoulders relative to the hips in boys also becomes apparent. Whereas the sitting height/stature ratio is similar for boys and girls until about 10 to 11 years of age, it becomes slightly higher in girls at adolescence.

Inferences about the timing and magnitude of the adolescent growth spurt in different body dimensions cannot accurately be made from cross-sectional growth studies. As initially suggested by Boas (1892), first applied by Shuttleworth (1937), theoretically based and explained by Tanner (1951), and eventually made available by Tanner, Whitehouse, and Takaishi (1966), growth and growth velocities should be assessed by synchronizing them on biological milestones. The selection of these milestones seems to be of importance, as demonstrated by Tanner, Hughes, and Whitehouse (1981) and Beunen et al. (1988). Isometric muscular strength as measured by various techniques in different muscle groups increases linearly with chronological age from early childhood until about 15 years in girls, with no clear adolescent spurt (Asmussen, 1973; Malina, 1986b). The pattern of maximal strength development in girls is not clear. The maximal velocity in strength development occurs more often after the peak height velocity in girls, but there is considerable variation although, on the average, greater gain in strength is made during the pubertal period than during either the prepuberal or postpuberal period (Faust, 1977). In Dutch girls a clear adolescent spurt in upper body strength is seen following the peak height velocity (Kemper & Verschuur, 1985a). During childhood sex differences are small but consistent. With increasing age during adolescence the differences are magnified, so that after 16 years of age, few girls perform as well as the boys' average (Jones, 1949).

Cross-sectional analyses of other motor abilities such as explosive strength, functional strength, trunk strength, (muscular endurance) and speed also show an improvement in average performances from childhood through adolescence. The performances in girls increase only to about 13 or 14 years of age, with little subsequent improvement (Branta, Haubenstricker, & Seefeldt, 1984). Some evidence suggests that the plateau of performances of adolescent girls in explosive strength and running speed has shifted to a slightly older age in more recent studies (Haubenstricker & Seefeldt, 1986). During adolescence, the performances of boys exceed those of girls and the differences become larger with age. An exception is flexibility; girls show greater levels of flexibility at virtually all ages (Haubenstricker & Seefeldt, 1986; Merni, Balboni, Bargellini, & Menegatti, 1981).

In a recent comprehensive review of the developmental aspects of maximal aerobic power, Krahenbuhl, Skinner, and Kohrt (1985) plotted values from 68 studies of clinically normal, untrained children and youths relative to chronological age. In girls, absolute $\dot{V}O_2max$ increases from about 1.0 L • min^{-1} at 6 years to about 2.0 L • min^{-1} at about 14 years of age. Subsequently, $\dot{V}O_2max$ declines with age in girls. When $\dot{V}O_2max$ is expressed relative to body weight it gradually decreases from about 52 ml • min^{-1} • kg^{-1} at 6 years to 40.5 ml • min^{-1} • kg^{-1} at 16 years. From the available evidence collected in longitudinal studies, Beunen and Malina (1988) concluded that in girls the data is not sufficient to offer generalizations about the occurrence of a growth spurt in maximal oxygen uptake. In boys, however, a growth spurt is reached near the time of peak height velocity.

Early investigations have shown that for a given work load there is a reduction in the intensity of the adaptive reaction with growth. Thus, for a given work load, the heart beats slower and the respiratory frequency is reduced with age (Bouchard, Thibault, & Jobin, 1981). This is reflected in the increase in PWC170 with age. Although there is some indication that in girls at puberty there is a decrease in PWC170 expressed per unit of body weight, this is not an inevitable accompaniment of maturation. For instance, in studies of girls receiving a vigorous physical education program a small increase is seen in PWC170/kg from 12 to 15 years of age (Shephard, 1978). The sex differences in PWC170 are already present at 5 to 6 years, increase somewhat with age and become most apparent at 12 to 13 years (Mocellin, Rutenfranz, & Singer, 1971). In each sex systolic and diastolic blood pressure increases with age from childhood to adolescence without evidence of a pubescent spurt (Woynarowska, Mukherjee, Roche, & Siervogel, 1985; Malina & Roche, 1983).

Lung function as measured by vital capacity and forced expiratory volume is related to the size of the child, and in most series is better described by stature than by other anthropometric variables (Cotes, 1979; Cotes, Dobbs, Hall, Heywood, & Laurence, 1979). Forced vital capacity and forced expiratory volume in girls increases with age and shows a spurt coincident with or after the growth spurt in height (Lange-Andersen et al., 1984). Boys have consistently higher values than girls. However, when forced expiratory volume is expressed as a percentage of vital capacity, girls have higher values than boys (Lange-Andersen et al., 1984; Kemper & Verschuur, 1985b).

Age Changes in Growth and Performance in Flemish Girls

Growth curves supply information about the growth and growth patterns shown by the different measurements and by physical performance test results; they are thus of the utmost importance for the evaluation of a fundamental process in the lives of human beings. For the period under study, the growth attained for the different measurements, the growth velocities and accelerations or decelerations can be followed. It is evident, however, that information about individual growth and growth patterns can best be obtained from longitudinal or mixed longitudinal studies. The timing and size of growth acceleration and deceleration patterns can differ strongly among individuals; therefore, cross-sectional reference data can only outline and not specify the individual model. The present reference data should thus be used to evaluate the status of a girl of a given age.

The growth curves of the anthropometric dimensions, skeletal maturity, lung functions, cardiorespiratory characteristics, and motor performance capacities were constructed as described in the section on data quality evaluation and data processing. As mentioned earlier, all data was collected within a one-week period. The chronological age of the subjects was calculated from the date of birth and the date of examination of the motor tests. Girls between 6.00 years and 6.49 years were considered as 6-year-old girls and those between 6.50 and 6.99 as 6.5 years old. In Table 9.1 the number of observations for each age category are given.

For each growth curve the percentiles P3, P5, P10, P25, P50, P75, P90, P95, and P97 are given. Considering the large number of observations in each age group, even the precision of the most extreme percentiles is fairly high: 94% if the observations are situated between P3 and P97, and 50% between P25 and P75. Together with the median (P50), these percentiles graphically form growth channels each comprising 2%, 5%, 15%, 25%, 25%, 15%, 5% and 2%. Only 3% of the observations are situated above P97 and below P3. It can be expected

Table 9.1 Number of Observations for Each Age Category

Age category	*n*
6.0 (6.00-6.49)	262
6.5 (6.50-6.99)	346
7.0 (7.00-7.49)	354
7.5 (7.50-7.99)	341
8.0 (8.00-8.49)	363
8.5 (8.50-8.99)	401
9.0 (9.00-9.49)	409
9.5 (9.50-9.99)	400
10.0 (10.00-10.49)	367
10.5 (10.50-10.99)	419
11.0 (11.00-11.49)	389
11.5 (11.50-11.99)	396
12.0 (12.00-12.49)	358
12.5 (12.50-12.99)	410
13.0 (13.00-13.49)	483
13.5 (13.50-13.99)	416
14.0 (14.00-14.49)	456
14.5 (14.50-14.99)	435
15.0 (15.00-15.49)	395
15.5 (15.50-15.99)	347
16.0 (16.00-16.49)	399
16.5 (16.50-16.99)	448
17.0 (17.00-17.49)	412
17.5 (17.50-17.99)	340
18.0 (18.00-18.49)	175

that a girl follows such a growth channel, but at periods of acceleration or deceleration, such as the pubertal growth spurt, marked deviations from such a channel can be observed. These deviations occur due to the child's individual time clock, which specifies the occurrence of these maturational events. A girl can experience an early pubertal growth spurt and show increased height velocities at the age of eight or nine.

The following graphs can thus be used to evaluate the girl's present status and to detect abnormalities. Any value below P3 or above P97 can be considered as suspect. For height, for example, such a girl should be followed and remeasured in order to evaluate the course of her growth process. For the sum of skinfolds, for example, a value above P75 can be considered as already at risk to develop adiposity. Furthermore, the reference data presented herein can be used to assess the health status of the Flemish female youth. From the graphs it can be deduced what percentage of girls is at risk of high blood pressure, obesity, or a poor health-related physical fitness level.

Somatic Growth and Skeletal Maturity

In general, all somatic dimensions increase throughout the entire period from 6 through 18 years. As adulthood approaches several dimensions level off and some even show a tendency to decline, such as suprailiac skinfold and biceps skinfold. The following description highlights the characteristics of the growth curves grouped by the main factors of the human somatic structure.

Weight, Height, and Lengths (Figure 9.1 and Figure 9.2)

The P50 values for weight increase curvilinearly from 6 years onward; from 11.0 years to 13.5 years the increase is steeper, and amounts to 5.0 to 6.0 kg/year. After 14.0 years the medians gradually level off. At each age level the distribution of weight is skewed; moreover, with increasing age the variability increases, more so for the high values. In absolute value the variability is highest at 13.5 and 14.0 years.

The medians for height increase linearly from 6.0 to 11.0 years, after which an acceleration (about 6 cm/year) is seen, followed by a leveling off from 13.0 years onward, reaching a value of 164.2 cm at 18 years. At each age level the P3 and P97 values are symmetrically situated around the P50 values. The variability increases somewhat until puberty. For all other lengths (i.e., leg length, sitting height, trunk height, acromial height, and forearm length), a similar trend is observed. For sitting height and trunk height an increased growth is observed between 12.5 and 14.5 years and for forearm length between 12.5 and 14 years. For leg length a linear increase is seen until 12.0 years, after which the growth curve levels off. At all age levels sitting height is markedly greater than leg length. The difference is 10.2 cm at 6 years, and remains at about the same level until 9 years. Thereafter the difference decreases and is smallest at 12 years, reflecting the earlier adolescent spurt in leg length rather than in sitting height. After 13 years the difference between sitting height and leg length increases and amounts again to 10.3 cm at 18 years.

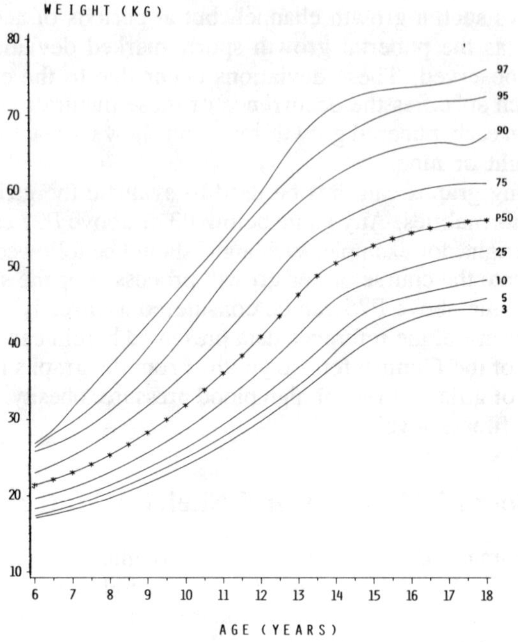

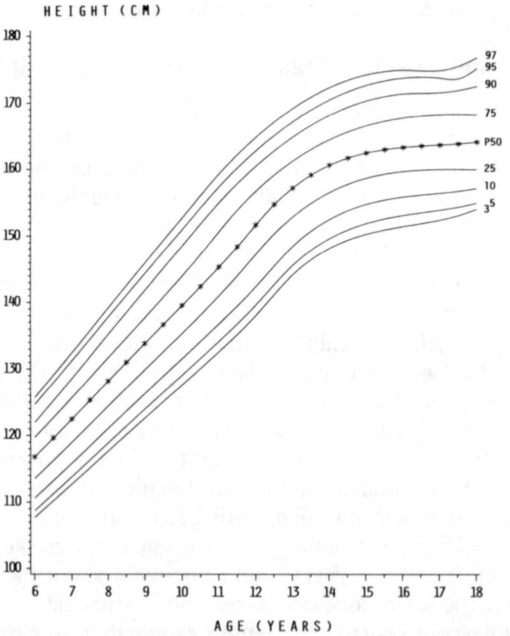

(Cont.)

Figure 9.1. Percentile distribution of Flemish girls 6.0 to 18.0 of age by weight and height, sitting height, and trunk height.

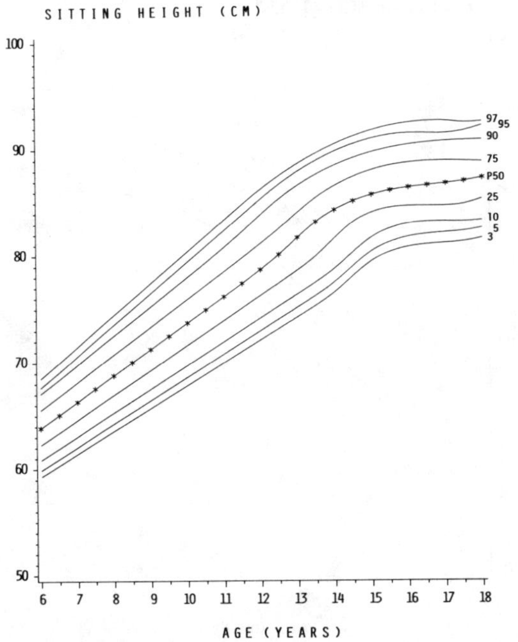

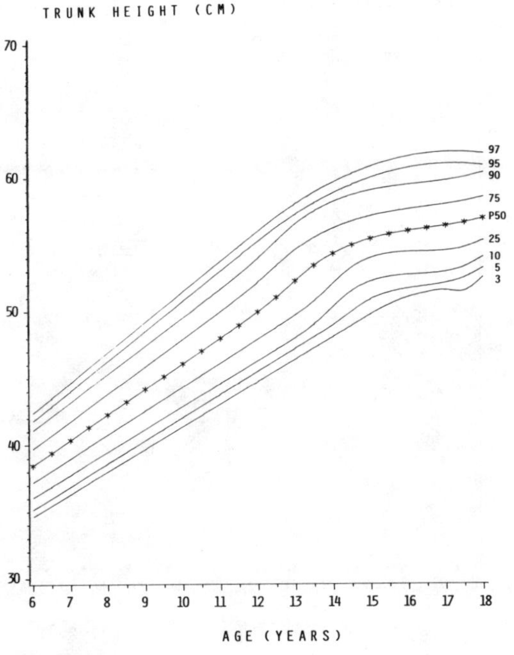

Figure 9.1. (Continued)

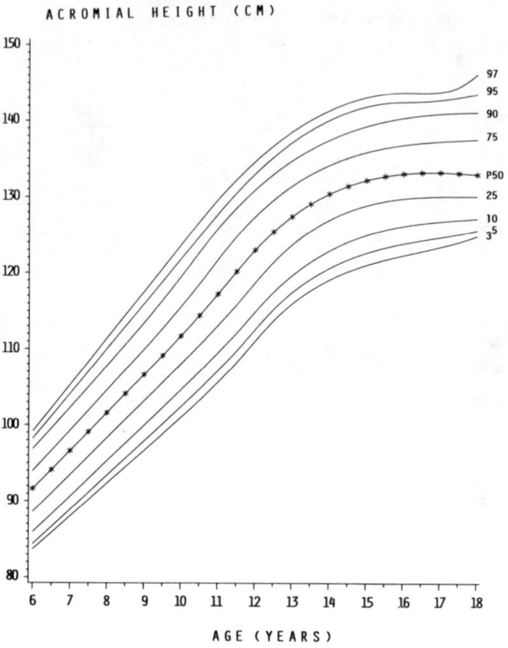

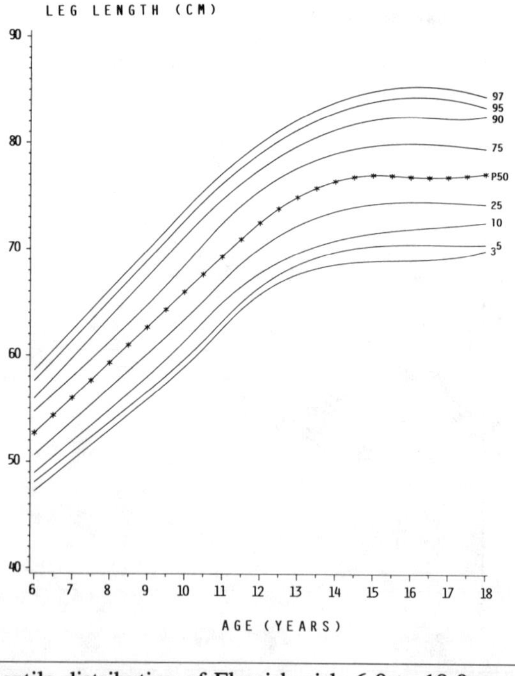

(Cont.)

Figure 9.2. Percentile distribution of Flemish girls 6.0 to 18.0 years of age by acromial height, leg length, and forearm length.

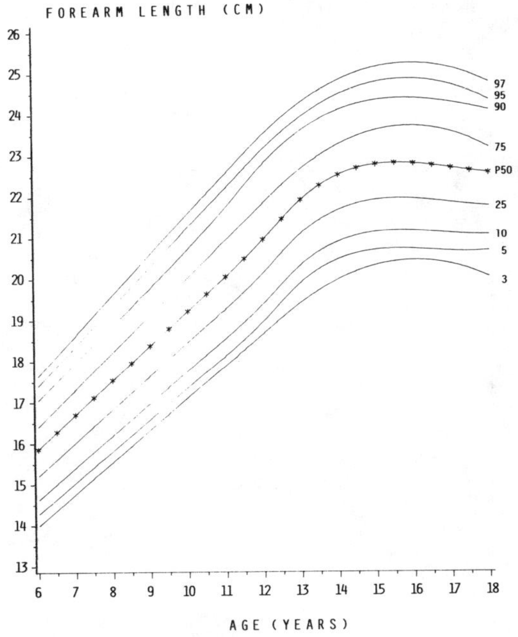

Figure 9.2. (Continued)

Head Dimensions (Figure 9.3)

Head length and head width slightly increase from 6.0 to 14.0-14.5 years, after which head width reaches a plateau and head length gradually levels off. The total increase amounts to 0.9 cm in head length and 0.8 cm in head width. The head circumference increases linearly from 50.7 cm at 6.0 years to 54.1 at 15 years, after which a plateau is reached. During childhood the P97 and P3 values are symmetrically situated around the medians; at puberty some asymmetry is seen toward the higher values. The variability also increases somewhat until puberty.

Trunk Breadths (Figure 9.4)

Biacromial and bicristal diameters increase linearly from 6.0 years until 12.0 years for biacromial diameter and until 10.5 years for bicristal diameter. Thereafter a growth spurt is seen, which is more marked for bicristal diameter. An increase of 3.8 cm over a period of 3.0 years is observed for bicristal diameter with an increase of 2.5 cm over a period of 2.5 years for biacromial diameter. After this period of increased growth, the biacromial diameter curve forms a plateau, whereas the curve for bicristal diameter still increases somewhat. At 18 years biacromial diameter is 35.2 cm and bicristal diameter 27.2 cm. The distributions of both trunk dimensions are rather symmetric during childhood but are asymmetric during adolescence, first toward the higher values and thereafter toward

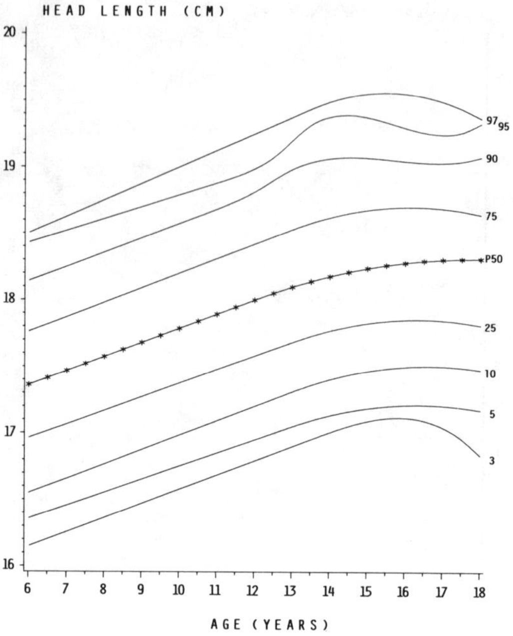

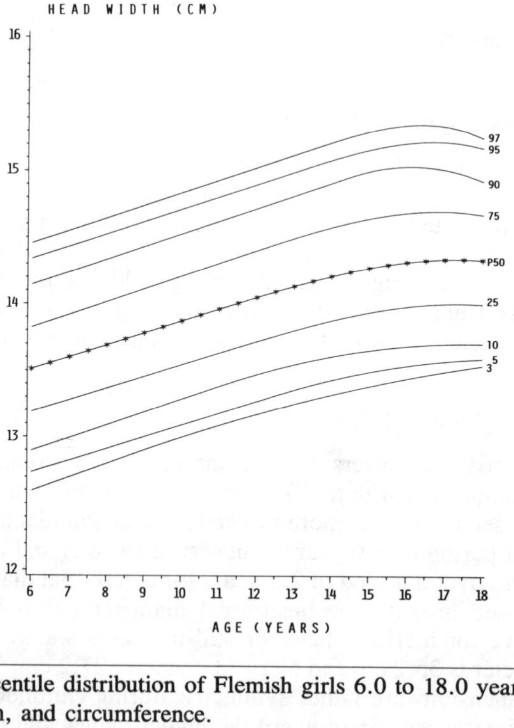

(Cont.)

Figure 9.3. Percentile distribution of Flemish girls 6.0 to 18.0 years of age by head length, width, and circumference.

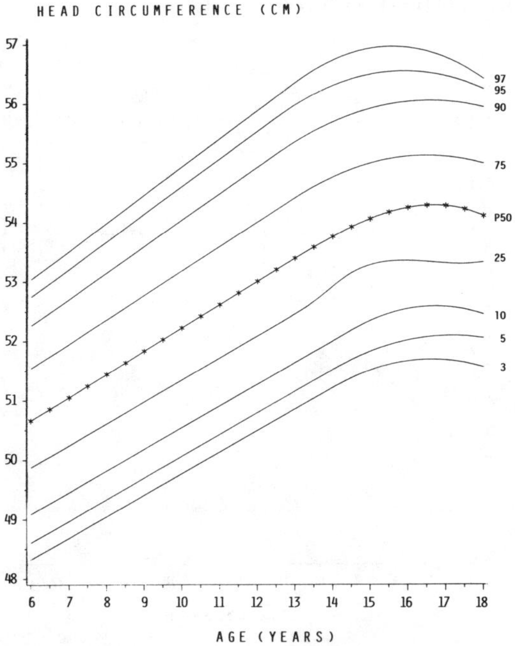

Figure 9.3. (Continued)

the lower values. The highest variability is found during the pubertal years. Chest width increases curvilinearly from 6.0 to 11.5 years, then growth increases until 14.5 years, after which a plateau is observed. At 18 years chest width amounts to 24.9 cm. The distribution is asymmetric, with highest variability during puberty.

Bone Diameters (Figure 9.5)

Both bone diameters increase linearly until 10.0 to 10.5 years, after which a small acceleration is found followed by a plateau or small increase. Adult values are 6.02 cm for humerus width and 8.5 cm for femur width. Humerus diameter is symmetrically distributed during childhood and after puberty but not during puberty. Femur diameter distributions are asymmetric at all age levels.

Limb Circumferences (Figure 9.6)

All limb circumferences increase curvilinearly until 11.0 to 11.5 years, then accelerate until 14.0 to 15.0 years, and thereafter they level off. At all age levels the distributions are markedly skewed toward the higher values. At 18 years the values for upper arm circumference extended and flexed, forearm circumference, thigh, and calf circumference are, respectively, 24.2 cm, 25.9 cm, 22.8 cm, 53.5 cm, and 33.9 cm.

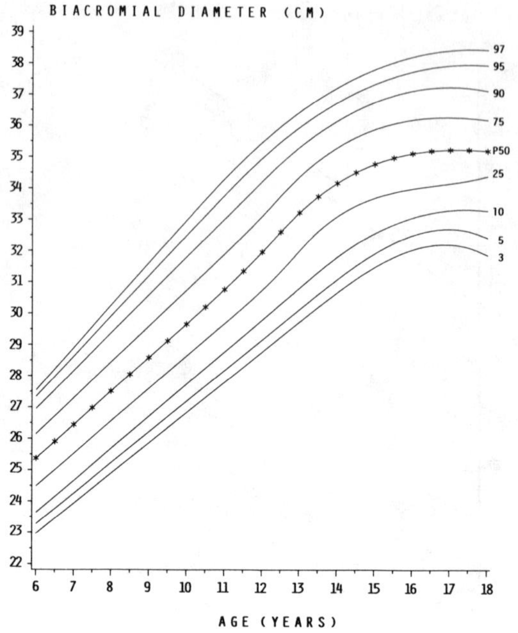

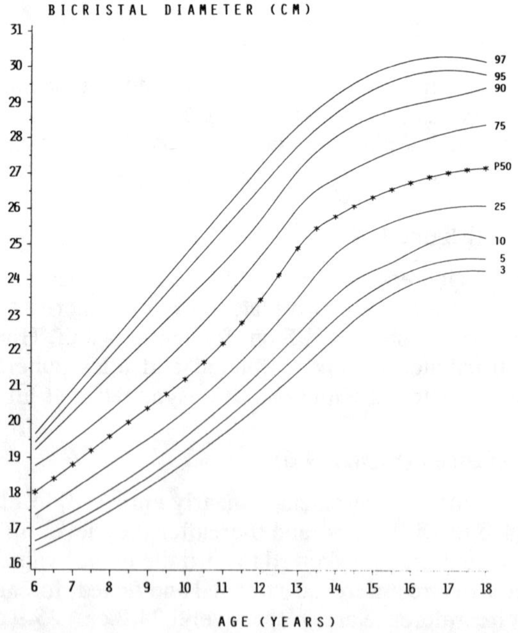

(Cont.)

Figure 9.4. Percentile distribution of Flemish girls 6.0 to 18.0 years of age by biacromial, bicristal, and chest widths.

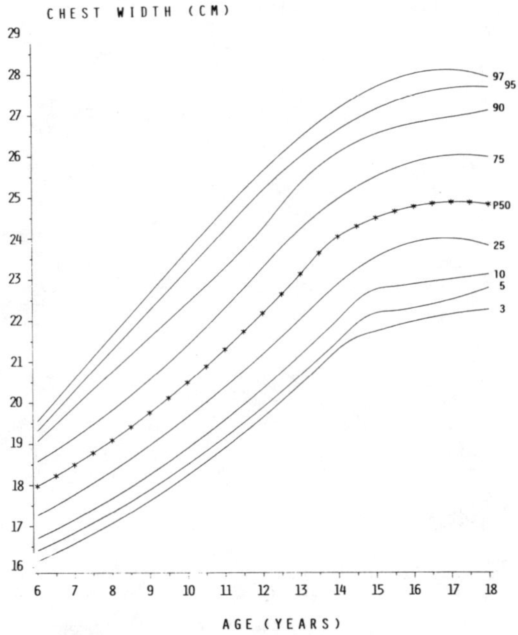

Figure 9.4. (Continued)

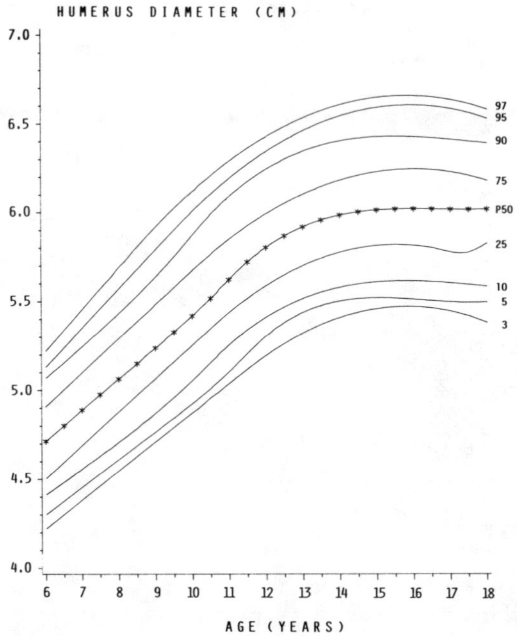

(Cont.)

Figure 9.5. Percentile distribution of Flemish girls 6.0 to 18.0 years of age by humerus and femur diameters.

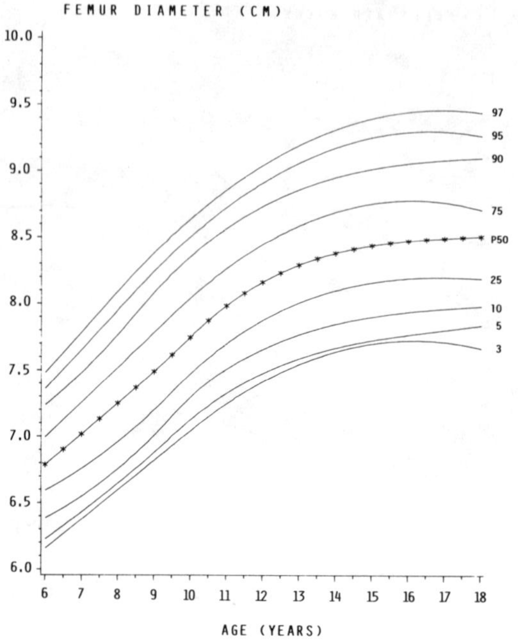

Figure 9.5. (Continued)

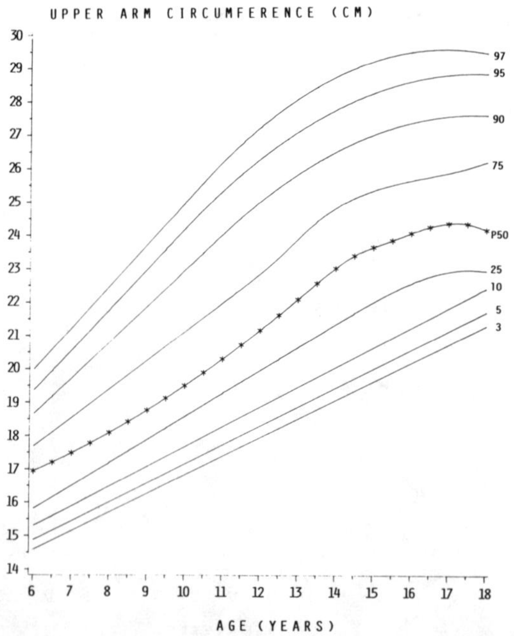

(Cont.)

Figure 9.6. Percentile distribution of Flemish girls 6.0 to 18.0 years of age by upper arm, upper arm flexed, forearm, thigh, and calf circumferences.

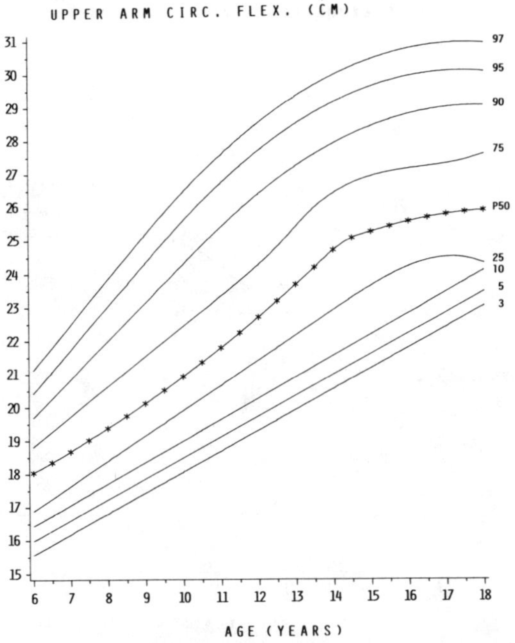

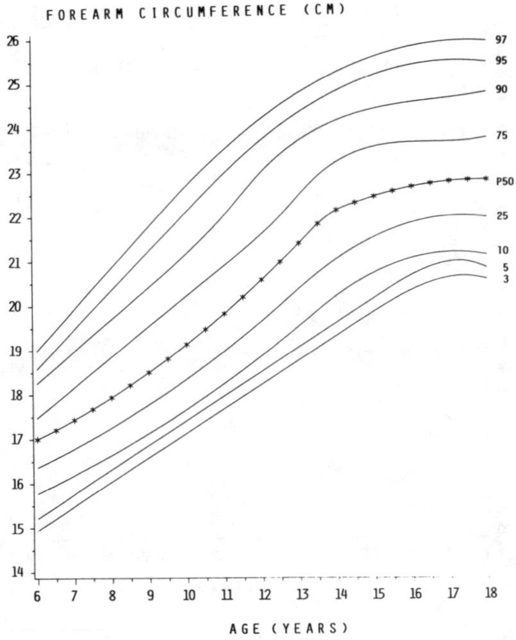

(Cont.)

Figure 9.6. (Continued)

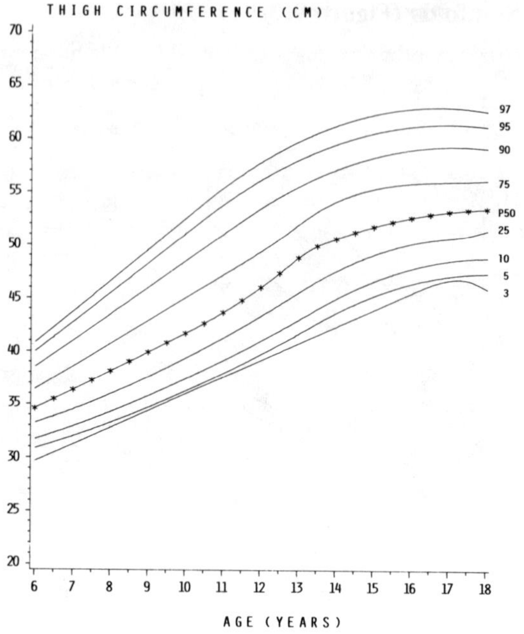

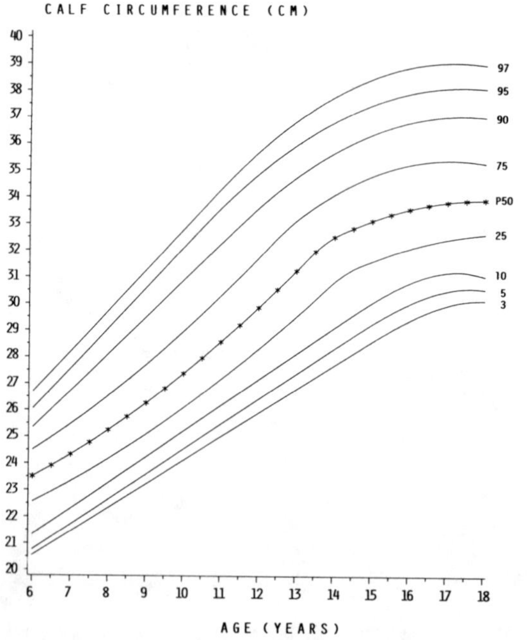

Figure 9.6. (Continued)

Subcutaneous Skinfolds (Figure 9.7)

As observed in so many other growth studies, skinfolds have a markedly skewed distribution at all age levels. Medians of subscapular skinfold remain nearly unchanged between 6.0 and 8 years, then increase and show an acceleration between 10.5 and 15.0 years, after which they level off. Suprailiac skinfolds increase from 6.0 years onward, show also an acceleration between 10.0 and 14.5 years, and then decrease from 16 years onward. Triceps skinfolds increase linearly until 9.5 years, then the increase is reduced to 0.2 mm/year. Between 13.0 and 15.5 years an acceleration is observed, followed by a plateau.

Still another growth pattern is seen for the medians of biceps skinfolds. A small linear increase is found from 6.0 years until 15.0 years and then a plateau, or even a small increase, is observed. The medians of calf skinfold increase from 6.0 to 10 years, accelerate until 15.0 years, and then gradually level off. At 6.0 years the triceps skinfold is the largest subcutaneous fatfold, followed by the calf, subscapular, biceps, and suprailiac skinfolds, in that order. At 8.0 years the median suprailiac skinfold is larger than the median biceps skinfold, and at 9.5 years the median suprailiac skinfold is larger than the median subscapular skinfold. At 11.0 years the median calf skinfold is larger than the median triceps skinfold. At 18.0 years the order is calf, triceps, subscapular, suprailiac, and biceps.

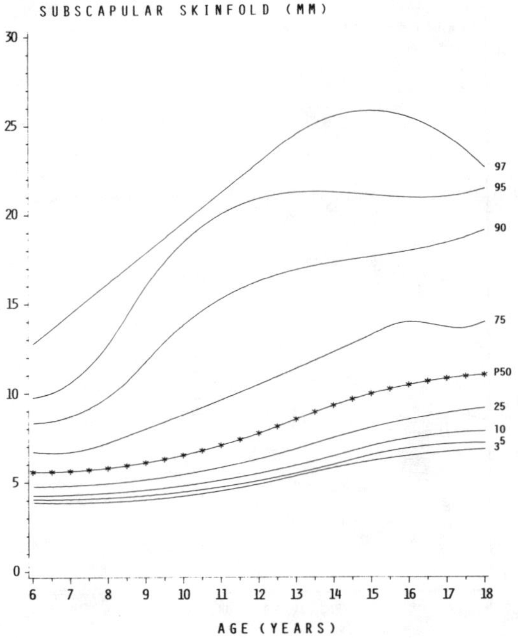

(Cont.)

Figure 9.7. Percentile distribution of Flemish girls 6.0 to 18.0 years of age by subscapular, suprailiac, triceps, biceps, calf, sum of three, and sum of five skinfolds.

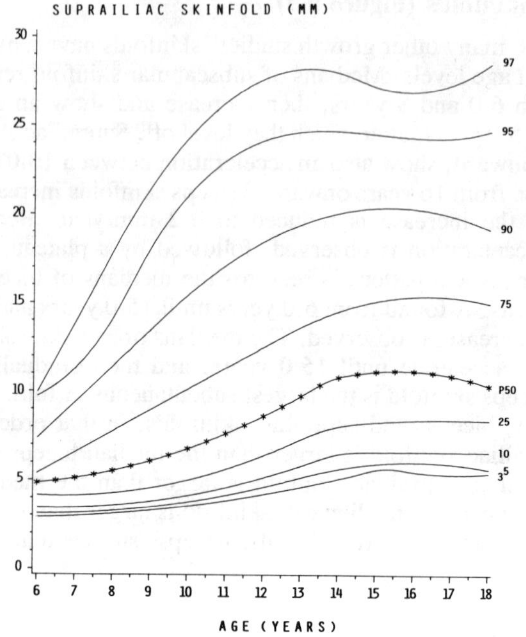

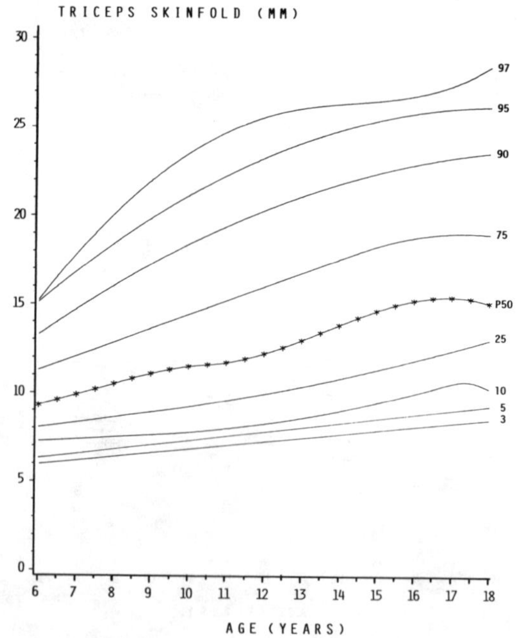

(Cont.)

Figure 9.7. (Continued)

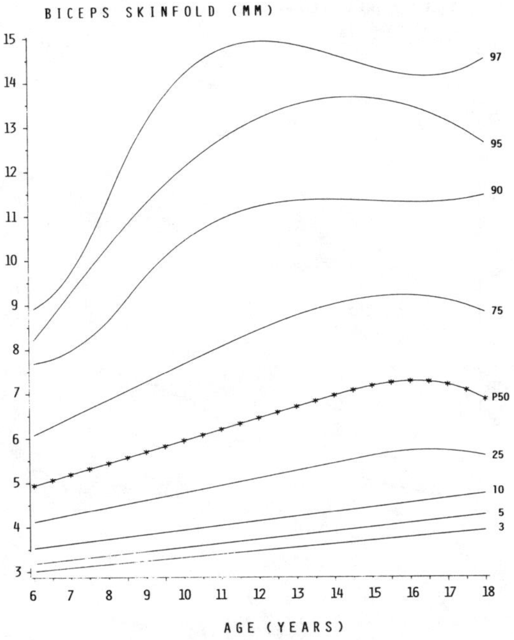

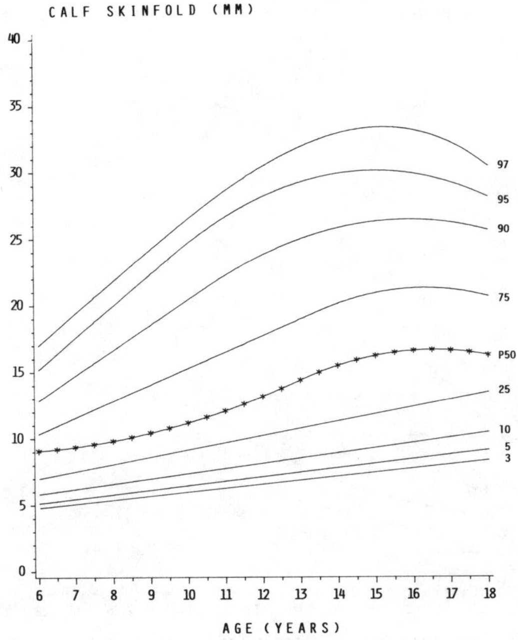

(Cont.)

Figure 9.7. (Continued)

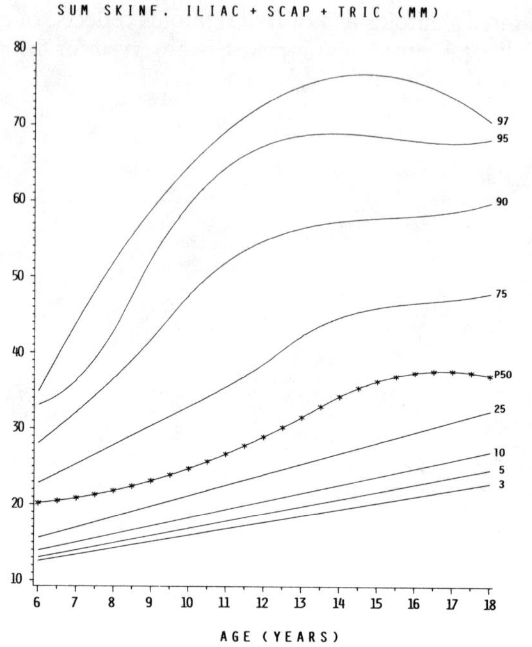

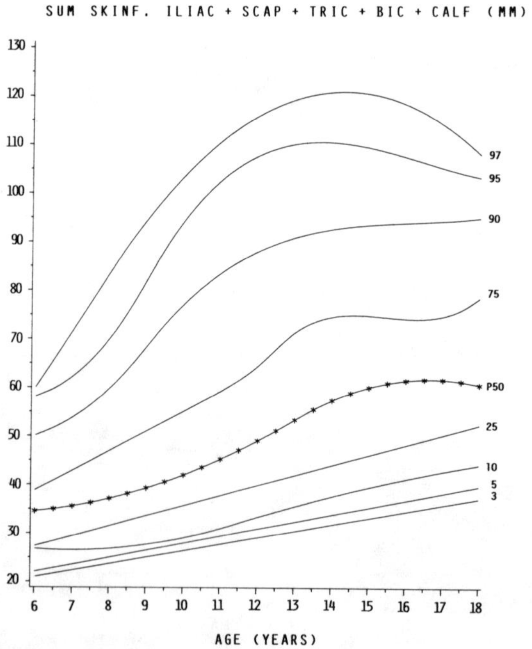

Figure 9.7. (Continued)

The sum of three skinfolds and of five skinfolds reflects, of cours
previously described. A curvilinear increase is observed for the media
by an acceleration and plateau or even a small decrease, mainly du
crease in suprailiac skinfolds. The sums of these skinfolds are cert
tools for the evaluation of adiposity in girls. Depending on the definition of obesity or adiposity one wishes to use, a cut-off value can identify those at risk. Similarly, these reference values can be used to identify girls who are at risk at the lower end of the scale and probably suffer from inadequate food intake due to dieting or other adverse conditions.

Skeletal Maturity Scores (Figure 9.8)

In accordance with the reference values presented by Tanner et al. (1975) and Tanner et al. (1983) a nonlinear scale was used to plot maturity scores against age. A transformation was used to obtain a better spread of the extreme percentiles at the attainment of adult maturity scores. The median CARP scores (carpal bones) increase curvilinearly from 6.0 years to 12.5 years when the maximum score is reached. The earliest maturing girls reach this endpoint as early as 10.0 years, whereas the latest 10% reach this endpoint at 14.5 years. The somewhat odd P97 curves are due to the scoring system. Also the RUS scores (radius,

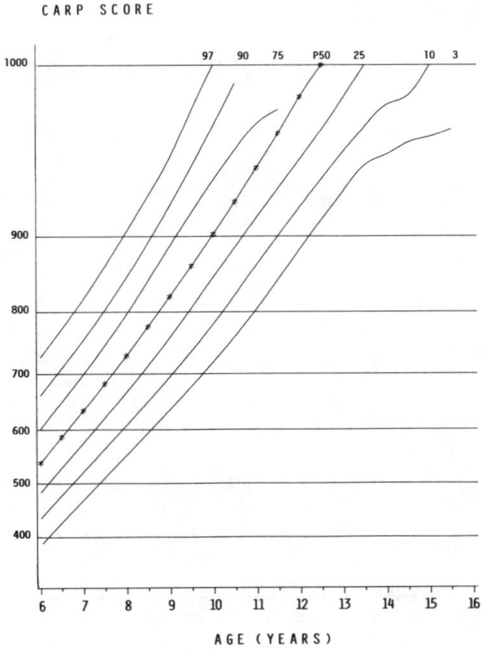

(Cont.)

Figure 9.8. Percentile distribution of Flemish girls 6.0 to 18.0 years of age by CARP, RUS, and TW2 scores.

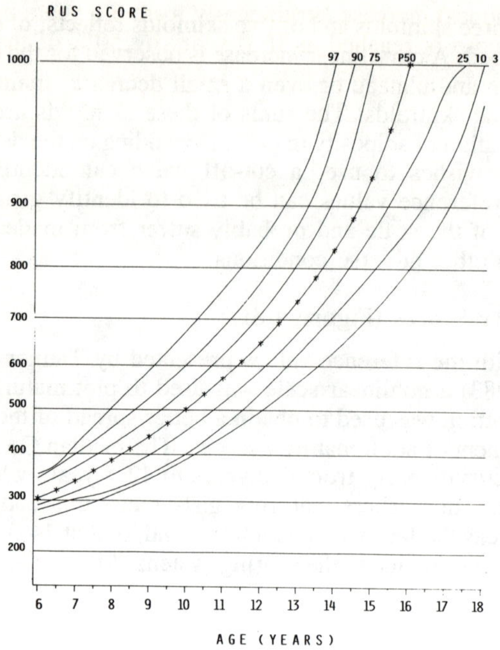

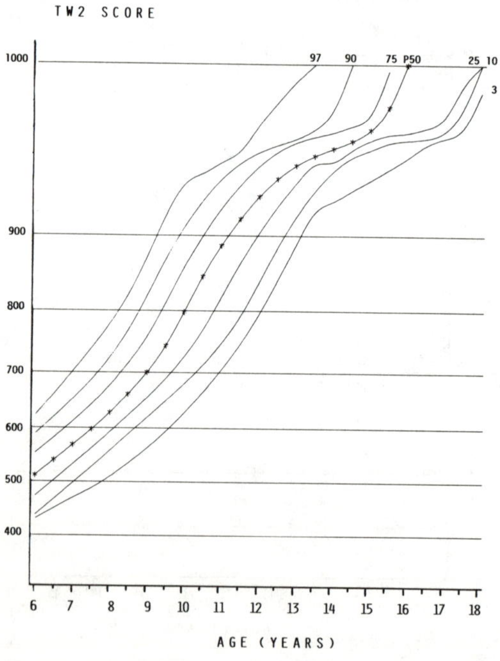

Figure 9.8. (Continued)

ulna, and short bones) increase curvilinearly from 6.0 years onward. The maximum maturity score is reached at 16.0 years by 50% of the girls, already at 14.0 years by the 3% of earliest maturing girls, and at 18.0 years by the latest 10%. The maturity scores of the 20 bones (TW2 scores) increase curvilinearly until 9.5 years, then accelerate until 11.0 years, after which a small increase is seen. Finally, a one-year acceleration period is once more observed. The adult status is reached at 16.0 years by 50% of the girls, whereas the 3% of earliest maturing girls reach this endpoint at 13.5 years, and the 10% of latest maturing girls reach this level at 18.0 years.

Lung Function, Cardiorespiratory, and Motor Performance Characteristics

Lung Function (Figure 9.9)

Medians of forced vital capacity increase curvilinearly until 14 years, slow down for 1.5 years, and thereafter increase again until 17.5 years. At 6.0 years about 1.0 L is expired, and at 18.0 years nearly 3.5 L. The distribution at each age level is fairly symmetrical in childhood. From 10.0 years onward the distribution is somewhat asymmetrical toward the higher values, but becomes rather symmetrical again at the end of adolescence. Peak flow medians show a linear increase until 11.5 years, followed by an acceleration and a leveling off from 14.5 years onward. At the upper limit of the age range some acceleration is once more noticed. The medians increase from 2.4 L at 6.0 years to 8.5 L at 18.0 years. Before 10.0 years the distribution is rather symmetrical, becomes asymmetrical toward the higher values and then toward the lower values. P25, P75, and P90 especially display more irregular patterns between 12.0 and 15.0 years.

Forced expiratory volume at 0.5 sec increases linearly until 12.5 years, then shows an acceleration over a short period and levels off until 18.0 years. The growth pattern of the expiratory volumes at 1 sec differs somewhat from the 0.5 values. During childhood a curvilinear increase is observed, followed by an acceleration and tapering off until 18.0 years. The medians for the 0.5 sec and 1 sec values increase from 0.7 L and 1.0 L at 6.0 years to 2.4 L and 3.3 L, respectively. At all age levels the distributions of the forced expiratory volumes at 0.5 sec and 1 sec are skewed toward the lower values.

Blood Pressure (Figure 9.10)

Median systolic blood pressures increase curvilinearly from about 83 mmHg to about 102 mmHg. The variability is high at the beginning of the period under study and declines somewhat thereafter, which results in an asymmetrical distribution toward the higher values from 10.0 years onward. Diastolic blood pressure displays a linear increase throughout the period studied. The medians range from 58 mmHg at 6.0 years to 7.0 mmHg at 17.0 years. The variability increases with age and the distribution gradually becomes skewed toward the higher values.

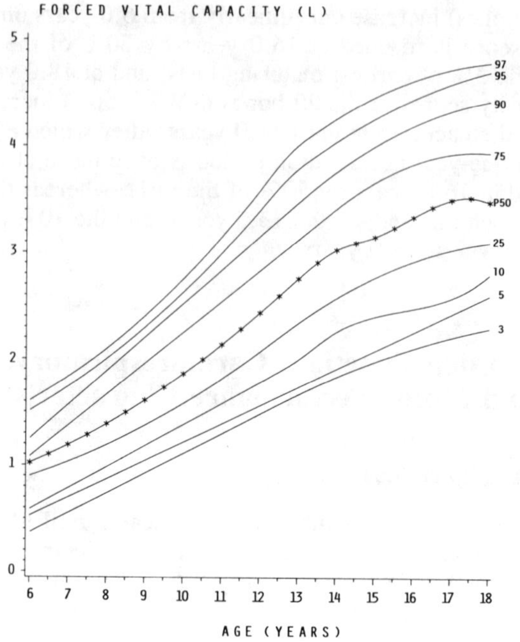

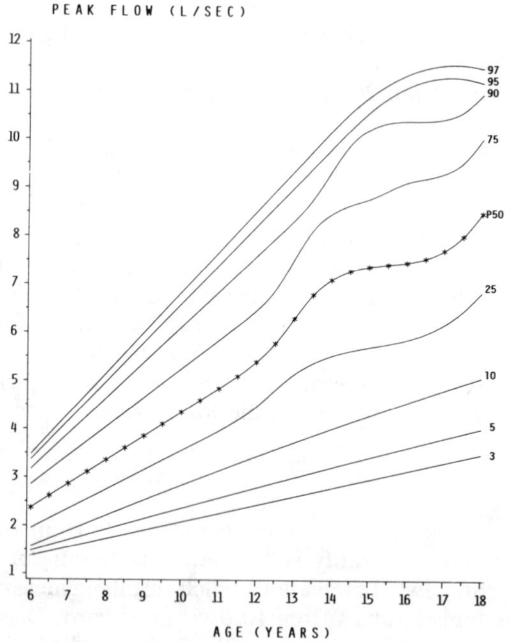

(Cont.)

Figure 9.9. Percentile distribution of Flemish girls 6.0 to 18.0 years of age by lung function parameters: forced vital capacity, peak flow, 0.5 and 1 sec forced expiratory volume.

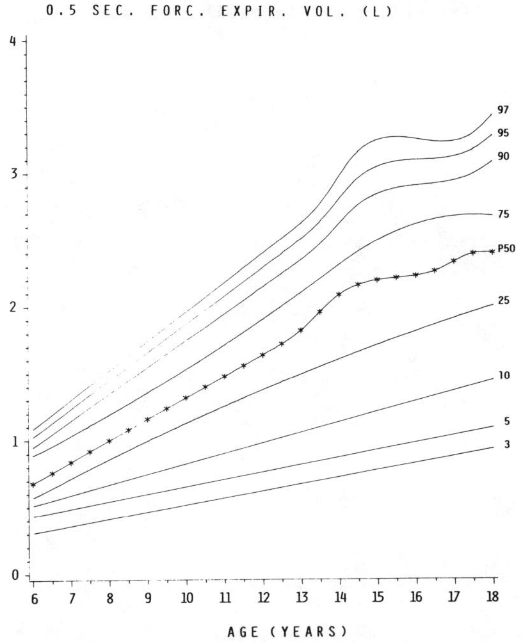

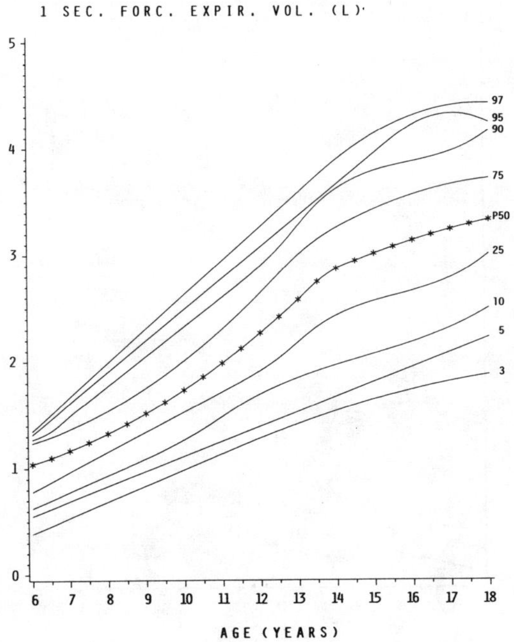

Figure 9.9. (Continued)

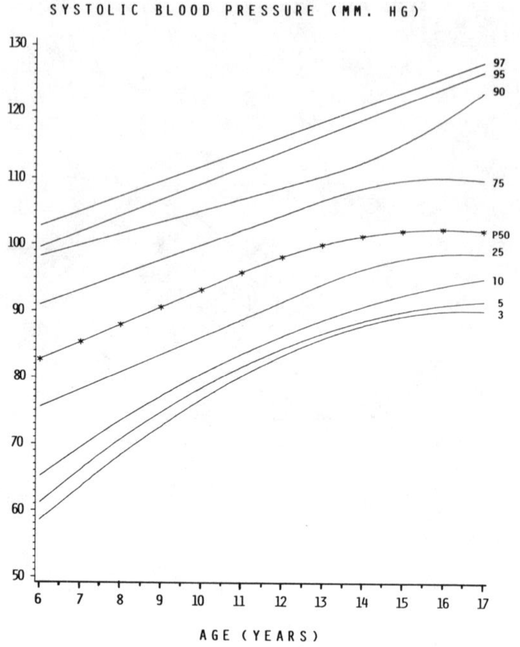

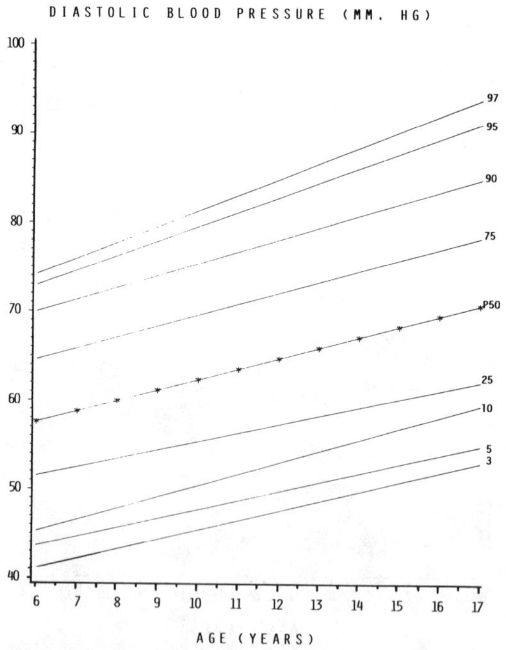

Figure 9.10. Percentile distribution of Flemish girls 6.0 to 17.0 years of age by systolic and diastolic blood pressure.

Pulse Rate (Figure 9.11)

Pulse frequency at rest and after a 1-minute step test is only observed from 9.0 years onward. Pulse frequency at rest in sitting position declines curvilinearly from 91 beats per minute at 9.0 years to 85 beats per minute at 18.0 years. The variability is high, and at all age levels the distribution is skewed toward the higher values. Pulse frequency after a 1-min step test surprisingly increases from 9.0 years until 15.5 years and then declines. The sum of the frequencies during 2 min increases from 179 beats per 2 min at 9.0 years to 201 beats per 2 min at 15.5 years and declines to 189 beats per 2 min at 18.0 years. Again the interindividual variability is high and the distribution at each age level is skewed toward the higher frequencies.

Cardiorespiratory Endurance (Figure 9.12)

Physical working capacity 150 (PWC150) increases linearly from about 171 kgm per minute at 6.0 years to 519 kgm per minute at 17.0 years. The variability increases also with age, which results in a more skewed distribution toward the higher values in the older age groups. Contrary to the trends observed for PWC150, the medians for PWC170 increase curvilinearly until 14.0 years after which the increase slows down. At 6.0 years the median PWC170 equals 210 kgm per minute and at 17.0 years 596 kgm per minute. Variability increases with age

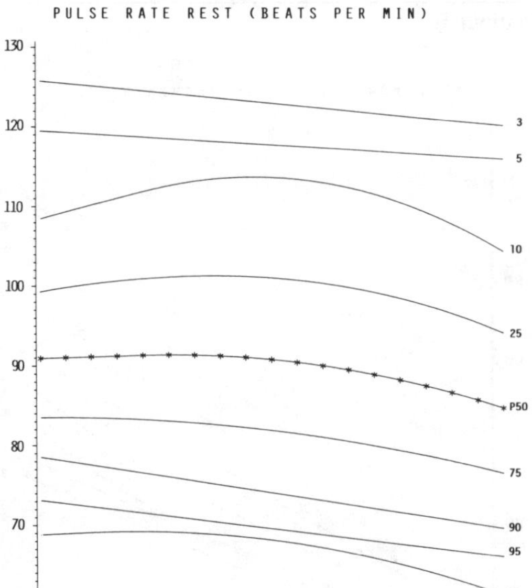

(Cont.)

Figure 9.11. Percentile distribution of Flemish girls 9.0 to 18.0 years of age by resting pulse rate and after 1-minute step test.

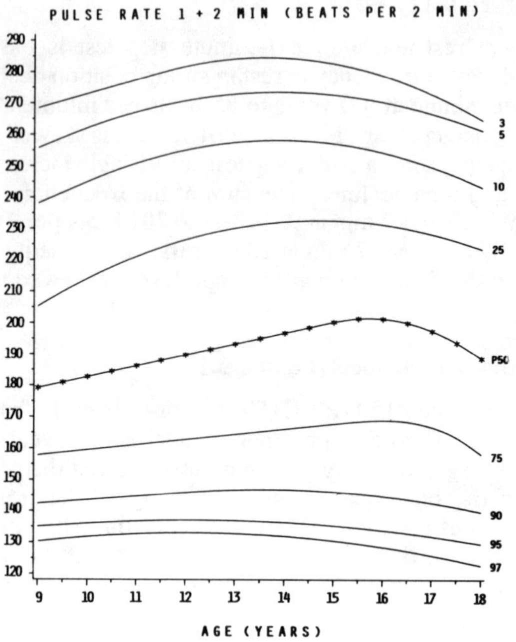

Figure 9.11. (Continued)

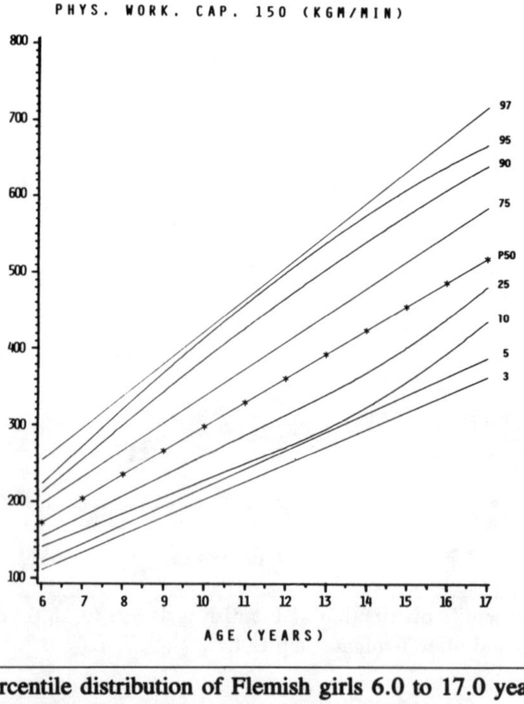

(Cont.)

Figure 9.12. Percentile distribution of Flemish girls 6.0 to 17.0 years of age by PWC150 and PWC170 and the 480-m shuttle run.

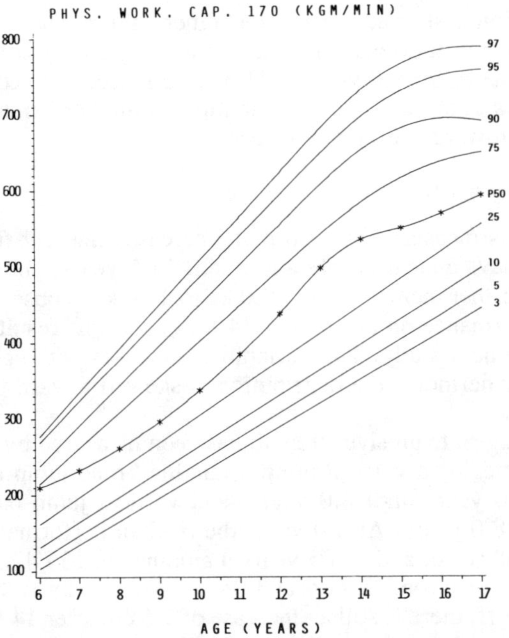

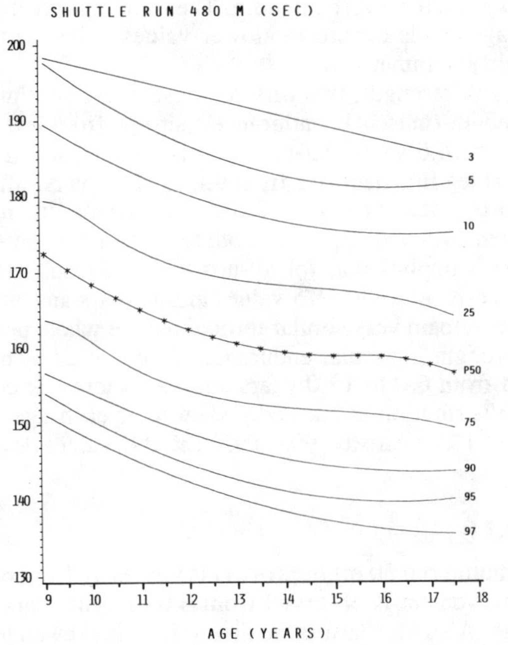

Figure 9.12. (Continued)

and the distribution is skewed toward the higher values. The time in seconds for the 480-m shuttle run shortens curvilinearly with age, with little or no improvement after 15.0 years. At 9.0 years, 172.5 sec are needed to cover the distance, and at 17.5 years 156.7 sec. The distribution of the performances at each age level is skewed toward the higher values.

Strength (Figure 9.13)

Static strength, as measured by arm pull, increases linearly from 6.0 years to 12.0 years, displays a clear acceleration until 14.5 years, and thereafter tapers off, although a further increase from 40.0 kg to 44.4 kg is observed. At 6.0 years the median performance on this task is 14.8 kg, and this result is nearly tripled over the period under study. The variability increases with age through to late adolescence. Furthermore, the distribution is skewed toward the higher values at all age levels.

At younger ages, explosive strength has been measured by a standing broad jump and thereafter by a vertical jump. Standing broad jump medians increase linearly from 6.0 years until 8.0 years, and vertical jump curvilinearly from 9.0 years until 18.0 years. At 6.0 years the median performance in a standing broad jump is 108.6 cm, and at 8.5 years it amounts to 136.4 cm. Vertical jump performance increases from 23.7 cm at 9.0 years to 33.2 cm. Although the median gradually tapers off, there is still an increase of 1.5 cm after 14.0 years, at which age the median equals 31.7 cm. The variability is quite high for both tests so that the P97 values at 6.0 years clearly surpasses the P50 values at 9.0 years for a standing broad jump, and likewise the P97 value at 9.0 years surpasses the P50 value at 14.0 years for a vertical jump. The standing broad jump distribution is skewed at all age levels toward the lower values, whereas the vertical jump distribution is fairly symmetrical.

As for explosive strength, two different tests were administered as a measure of trunk strength (muscular endurance): sit-ups from 6.0 to 9.0 years and leg lifts from 9.0 to 18.0 years. Sit-up medians increase linearly from 6.0 until 9.0 years, whereas leg lifts decrease from 9.0 to 12.0 years, after which a small curvilinear increase is observed until 17.0 years. The leg lifts medians at all age levels vary between 14.9 and 17.1. For both tests the inter-individual variability is very high, which implies that for sit-ups the best results (P97) obtained at 6.0 years still correspond to the P75 values at 9.0 years and, moreover, for leg lifts the P97 values remain very similar throughout the whole period under study.

Functional strength (muscular endurance) as measured by bent arm hang remains unchanged from 6.0 to 13.0 years and then increases curvilinearly until 18.0 years. The distribution is markedly skewed at each age level toward the higher values: after 13.0 years the P90, P95, and P97 values deviate further from the medians.

Speed (Figure 9.14)

Running speed (shuttle run 50 m) improves curvilinearly from 6.0 to 18.0 years, but the main improvement is observed from 6.0 to 11.0 years. The variability decreases with age. Also for this test the distribution is skewed toward the higher values. Speed of limb movement, as measured by plate tapping, improves curvilinearly throughout childhood and adolescence. At 6.0 years the median is 40 taps

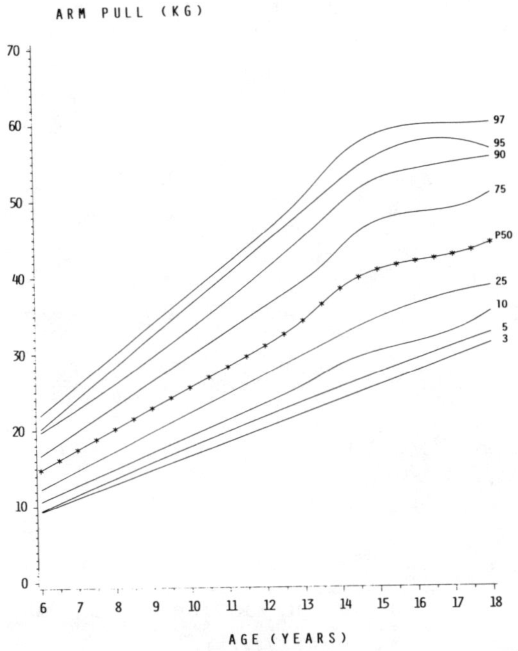

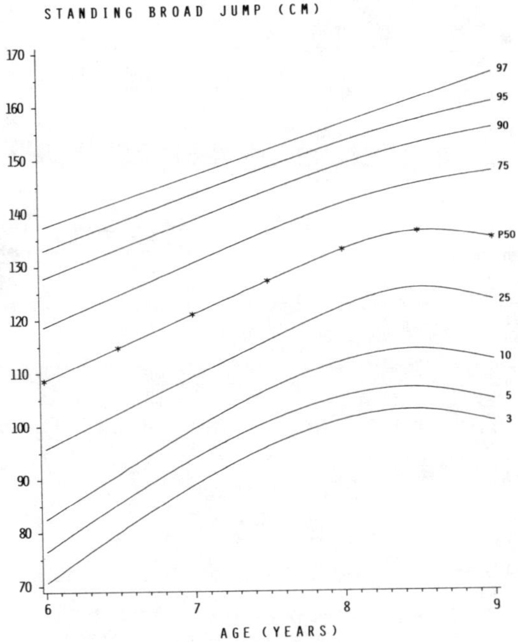

(Cont.)

Figure 9.13. Percentile distribution of Flemish girls 6.0 to 18.0 years of age by arm pull, standing broad jump, vertical jump, sit-up, leg lift, and bent arm hang.

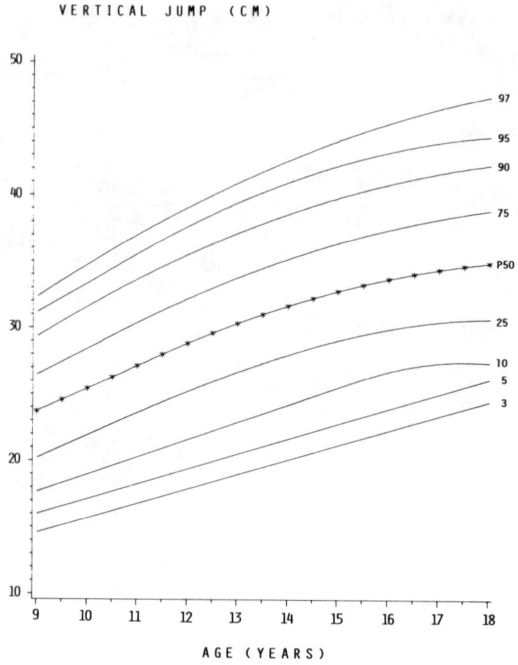

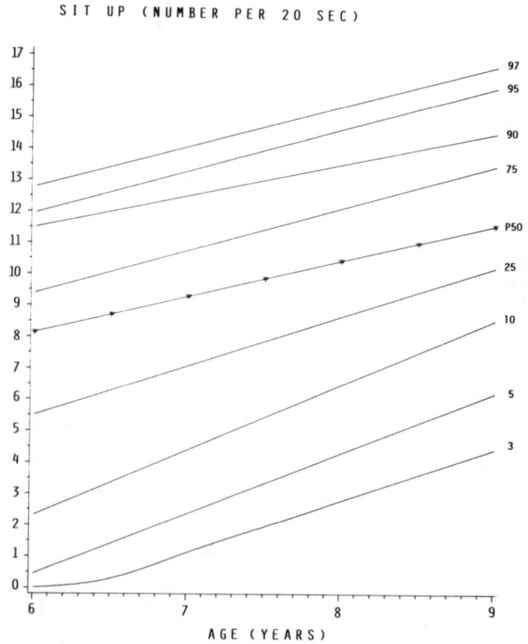

(Cont.)

Figure 9.13. (Continued)

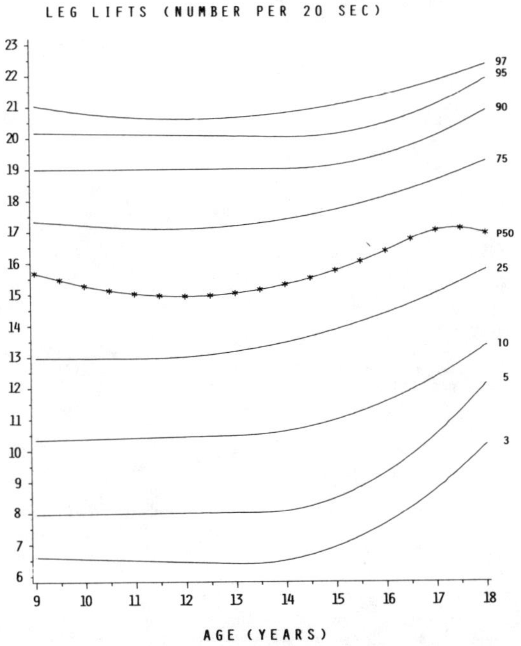

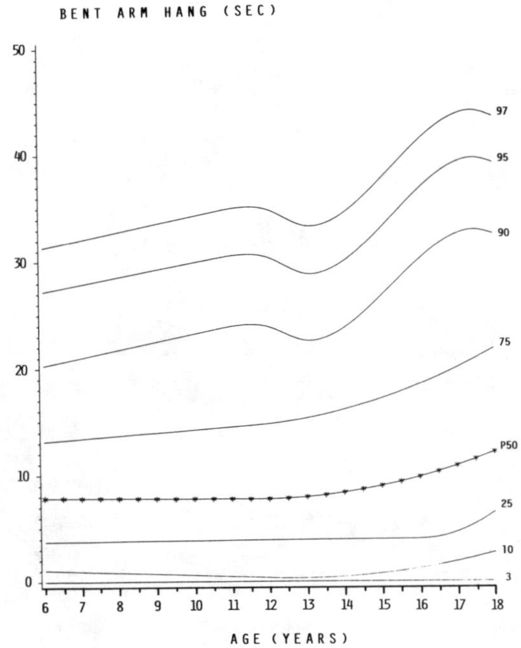

Figure 9.13. (Continued)

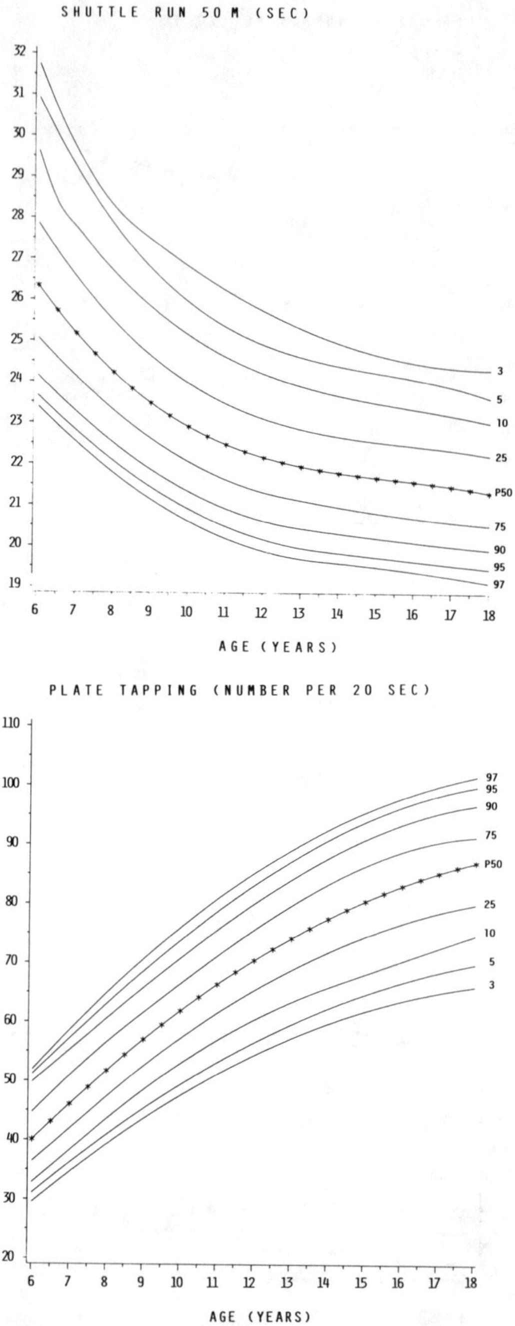

Figure 9.14. Percentile distribution of Flemish girls 6.0 to 18.0 of age by 50-m shuttle run and plate tapping.

and at 18.0 years it amounts to 91.4 taps. During childhood the distribution at each age level is rather symmetrical but becomes asymmetrical during adolescence and is skewed toward the lower values.

Flexibility (Figure 9.15)

Sit and reach medians decline with age until 11.5 to 12.0 years when a short acceleration is seen; thereafter the median tapers off. The median for 6.0-year-old girls corresponds to that of 13.5-year-old girls. The distribution is skewed toward the lower values at all age levels. Furthermore, the variability increases somewhat with age.

Balance (Figure 9.16)

Although the same test was used to measure total body balance, it was necessary to change the width of the balance beam for the younger age levels. From 6.0- to 9.0-year-olds medians for flamingo balance improve linearly with age, and the same holds true for the 9.0- to 18.0-year age range. The distributions are markedly skewed toward the higher values at each age level, especially for 8.0- and 9.0-year-old girls. For these age groups the test is apparently too easy for the best performing girls; large numbers of girls only reached a minimal score of one trial.

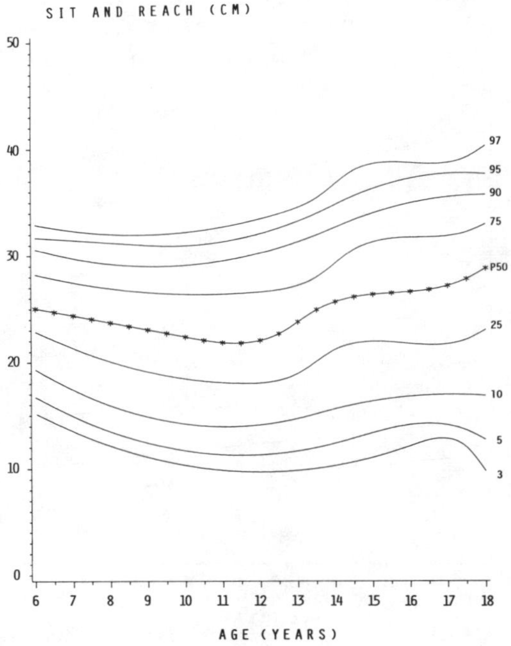

Figure 9.15. Percentile distribution of Flemish girls 6.0 to 18.0 years of age by sit and reach.

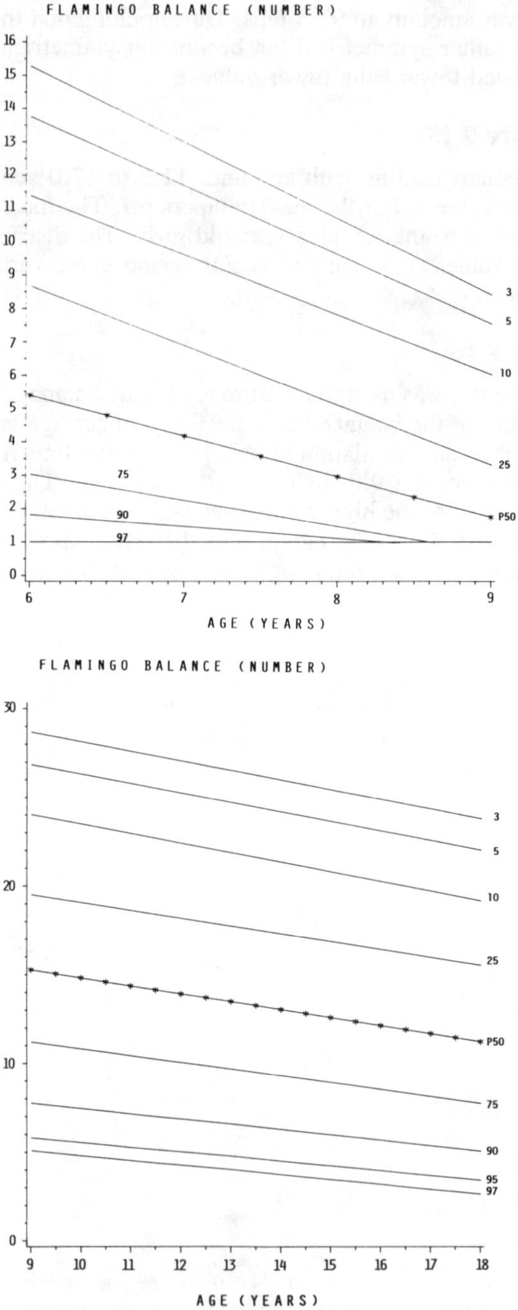

Figure 9.16. Percentile distribution of Flemish girls 6.0 to 9.0 and 9.0 and 18.0 years of age by flamingo balance.

Discussion and International Comparisons

Somatic Dimensions and Skeletal Maturity

Most trends observed in this large epidemiological study of Flemish girls correspond closely to what has been reported for other populations. Some characteristics of these growth patterns are interesting enough to be highlighted again. During childhood most body dimensions increase linearly with the exception of weight, chest width, and limb circumferences, which increase curvilinearly. Nearly all body dimensions show an adolescent growth acceleration that apparently occurs at different age levels. From these cross-sectional reference values it is, however, quite difficult to define the age at which these accelerations are maximal; moreover, the magnitude of these accelerations cannot be correctly estimated. A number of body dimensions also display a skewed distribution at each age level or during adolescence. Classical examples are of course subcutaneous skinfolds and weight, but limb circumferences and bone diameters are also rather skewed in their distributions. Similarly, biacromial and bicristal diameter show some skewness in their distribution during adolescence.

Although a large number of reference values for somatic dimensions have been published (Eveleth & Tanner, 1976), there is great variability in the measuring

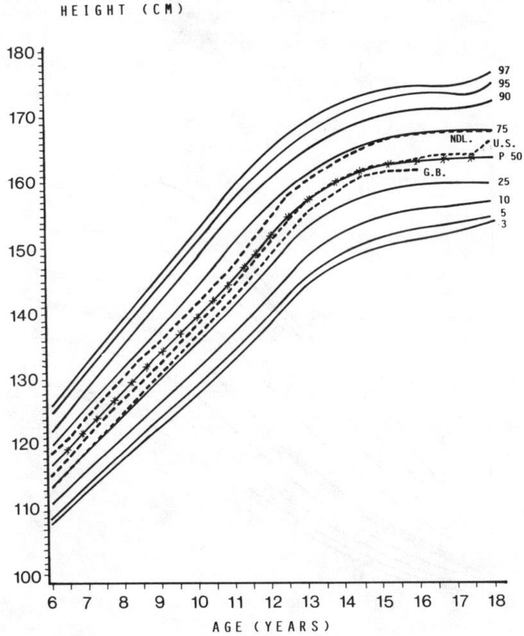

Figure 9.17. Percentile distribution of Flemish girls 6.0 to 18.0 years of age by height compared to medians from national samples of Great Britain (GB), The Netherlands (NDL) and the United States (US). Redrawn after Hamill et al., 1977; Roede & Van Wieringen, 1985; Tanner & Whitehouse, 1976.

techniques, which complicates comparative studies. The median values for height and weight of British (Tanner & Whitehouse, 1975), American (Hamill, Drizd, Johnson, Reed, & Roche, 1977), and Dutch (Roede & Van Wieringen, 1985) girls were plotted against the reference data of Flemish girls.

The medians for height of the British (GB) sample correspond to the P25 values of Flemish girls at 6.0 years, gradually approach the P50 values, but never reach the same values (Figure 9.17). The height of the United States (US) girls is somewhat smaller than that of Flemish girls but, from 13 years onward, the medians coincide exactly. Dutch (NDL) girls are larger at 6.0 years than their Flemish counterparts; with increasing age these differences are accentuated, so that at 18.0 years the medians of Dutch girls coincide with the P75 values of Flemish girls. This is surprising, since differences in measuring technique cannot explain this difference of 4 cm in the medians, which is about 0.7 *SD*. Furthermore, the data for the two studies were collected during the same period, so secular trends cannot account for these discrepancies. The reasons for these (in our opinion) enormous differences are unclear to us. As stated by Roede and Van Wieringen (1985), the Dutch population is most probably among the tallest on earth.

For weight, much smaller differences are found (Figure 9.18). Girls from Great Britain weigh somewhat less than Flemish girls until 14 years and thereafter surpass them. Medians of US girls are nearly identical with those of Flemish

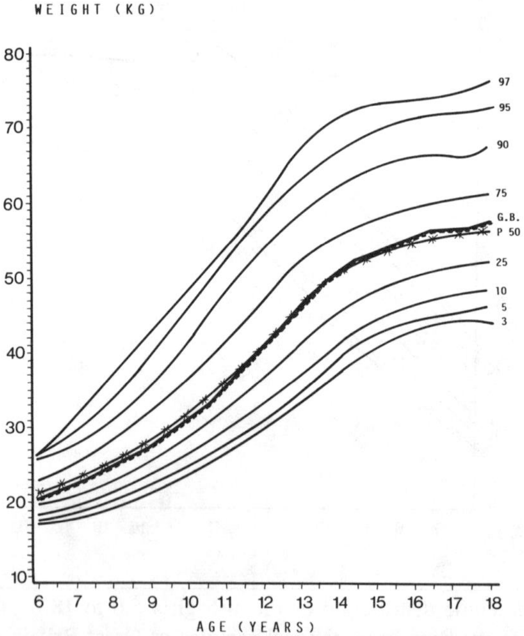

(Cont.)

Figure 9.18. Percentile distribution of Flemish girls 6.0 to 18.0 years of age by weight compared to medians from national samples of (a) Great Britain (GB), (b) The Netherlands (NDL), and (c) the United States (US). See note to Figure 9.17.

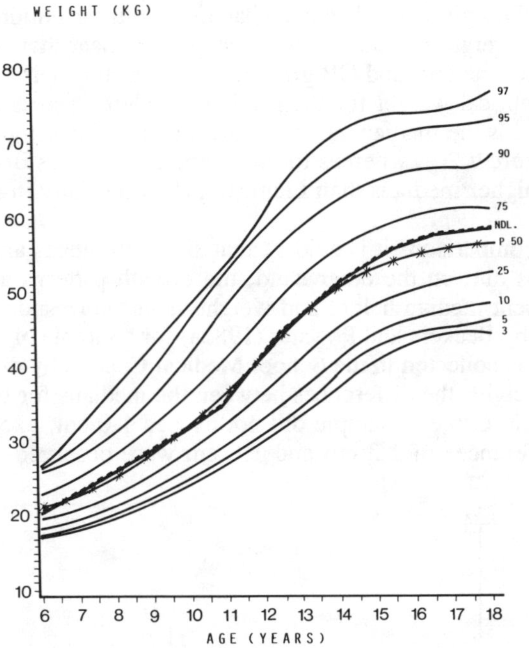

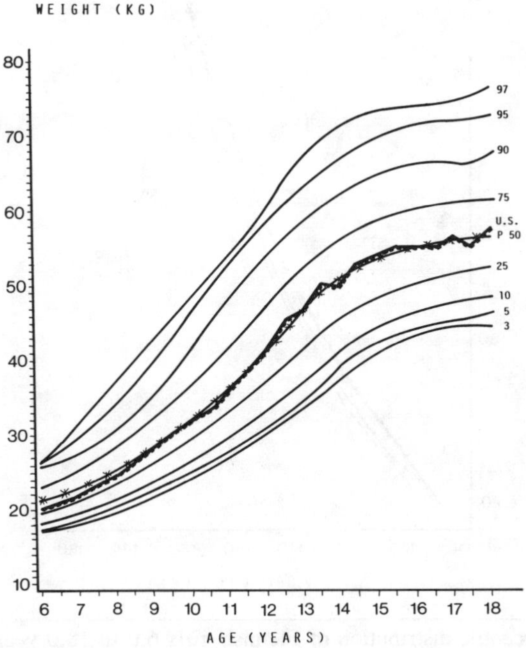

Figure 9.18. (Continued)

girls, whereas NDL girls weigh somewhat more during childhood and after 14.0 years. When weight is plotted against height it is clear that NDL girls have less weight for their height, and GB girls more weight for their height, whereas US girls have identical weight for their height to Flemish girls (Figure 9.19). For triceps skinfolds the median values of Flemish and British girls correspond quite closely (Figure 9.20), whereas for subscapular skinfolds British girls have at all age levels higher medians than Flemish girls, especially in their late teens (Figure 9.21).

From these comparisons it is evident that size differences are observed between populations but, on the other hand, the growth patterns are remarkably similar. The present median height and weight values correspond quite closely to those reported by Beckers and Pleysier (1982a) for a sample of 63,496 Belgian girls. The data was collected in the School Medical Centers by different anthropometrists. For height, the differences between the medians for our sample and the School Medical Centers' sample did not exceed 1.0 cm, except at two age levels where differences of 1.3 cm and 1.6 cm were observed.

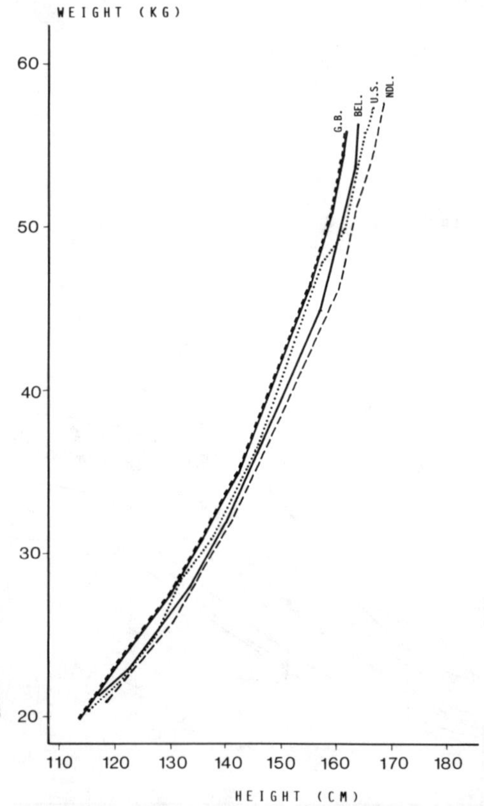

Figure 9.19. Percentile distribution of Flemish girls 6.0 to 18.0 years of age height by weight compared to medians from national samples of Great Britain (GB), The Netherlands (NDL), and the United States (US). See note to Figure 9.17.

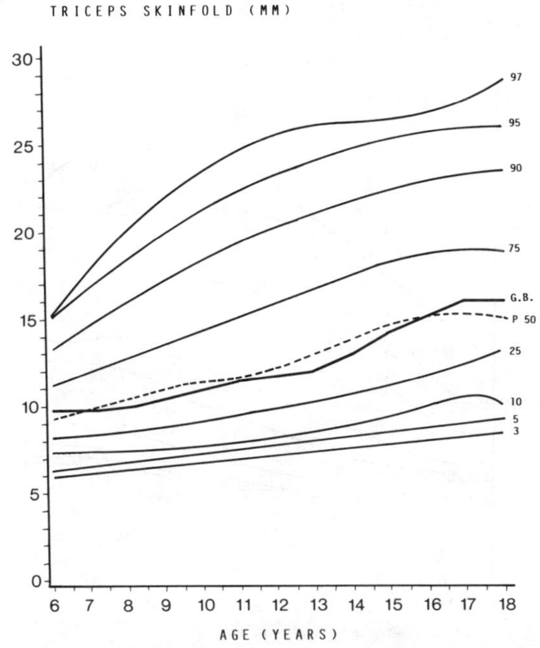

Figure 9.20. Percentile distribution of Flemish girls 6.0 to 18.0 years of age by triceps skinfold compared to medians from a national sample of Great Britain (Redrawn after Tanner & Whitehouse, 1975).

Similarly, at none of the age levels did the differences in the weight medians exceed 1.0 kg. Beckers and Pleysier (1982a) observed in young girls a secular increase in height over a 20-year period (1960-1980) of the order of 1.1 cm to 2.1 cm per decade, depending on the age level; for weight, the secular increase varied between 0.4 kg and 1.7 kg per decade over the same period. However, the same authors noticed that the secular increase in Belgian conscripts diminished from 2 cm/decade in the 1950 to 1959 and 1960 to 1969 period to only 1 cm/ decade in the 1970 to 1979 period (Beckers & Pleysier, 1980).

Radius, ulna, and short bones maturity scores (RUS scores) of Belgian girls exceed those of British girls (Tanner et al., 1983) at all ages until late puberty (Figure 9.22). Between 6 and 11.5 years the medians of the Belgian girls correspond to the P75 values of British girls, whereafter the P50 values gradually shift to the P50 values of the British girls so that, on the average, the adult maturity score is reached at the same age level. Similar trends, but at different age levels, are observed for carpal and 20-bone scores (Figures 9.23 and 9.24). This means that Belgian girls are, on the average, advanced in skeletal maturity status as compared to British girls, but on approaching adulthood their maturity status corresponds more and more. Also P97 and P3 values are situated at higher levels, although again on approaching adulthood the P3 values for the three maturity scores correspond closely. Lastly, at the youngest ages, the 20-bone scores and RUS scores of the Belgian girls show less variability than those of

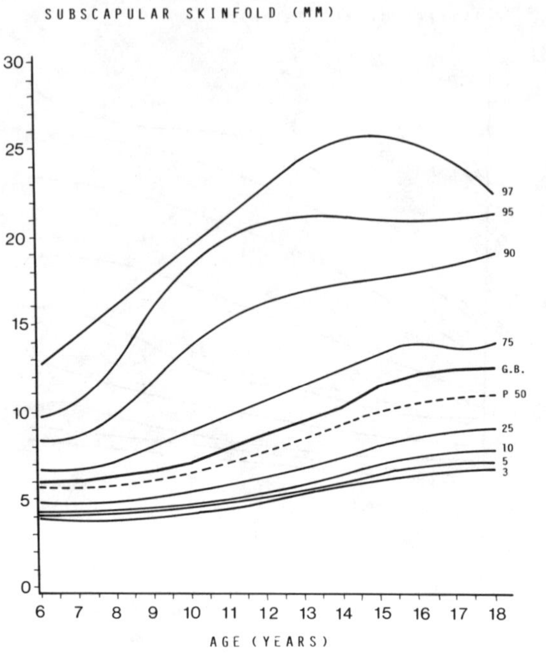

Figure 9.21. Percentile distribution of Flemish girls 6.0 to 18.0 years of age by subscapular skinfold compared to medians from a national sample of Great Britain. See note to Figure 9.20.

the British girls. The differences are probably a reflection of actual population differences, but it should be kept in mind that the British data were collected between 1946 and 1972.

Especially for the younger ages, for which most of the data were collected in the fifties, a positive secular trend can be expected. This is probably a major explanation of the larger differences at the younger age levels. The very high intra- and inter-observer reliability, as discussed earlier, is certainly not an important source of the differences between the two samples. This comparative study leads to the conclusion that skeletal maturity reference data should be revised regularly. This will certainly also lead to a more precise prediction of adult stature, since skeletal age is used as an important predictor in regression equations for prediction of adult height such as those provided by Tanner et al. (1983).

Cardiorespiratory Functions and Motor Performance

Although studies have been published presenting reference values for a diversity of cardiorespiratory and motor characteristics, it is often tricky to compare results. A major obstacle in comparing the physical performance capacities of different populations is the sometimes slight, but nevertheless important, difference in testing procedures. Even more important is the difference in the tests used to measure basic performance capacities. For this reason the comparisons that are made

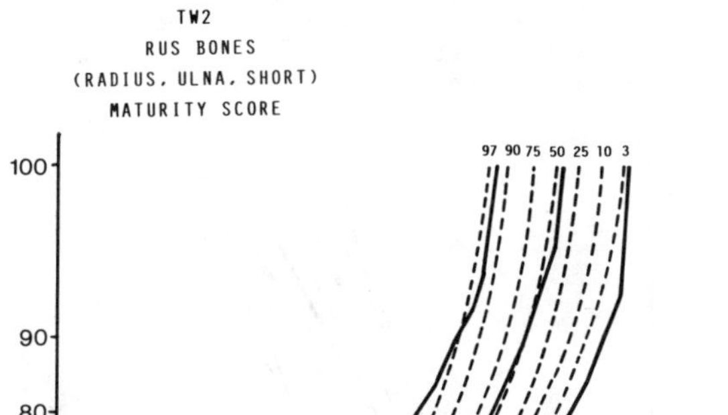

Figure 9.22. Percentile distribution of Flemish girls 6.0 to 18.0 years of age by RUS scores (TWII) compared to the distribution of British girls (GB) (Redrawn after Tanner et al., 1975).

are limited, and care was taken to select only those studies in which identical tests and comparable testing procedures were adopted.

Forced vital capacity of Norwegian girls systematically exceeds that of the Belgian girls at comparable ages (Lange-Andersen et al., 1984). Although the Norwegian girls are also somewhat taller at each age level, this difference in stature cannot account for the higher lung capacity in Norwegians. Similarly, forced expiratory volume after 1 second is higher in Norwegian girls.

Seated systolic blood pressures of girls measured serially in the Fels Research Institute (Roche et al., 1979; Woynarowska et al., 1985) correspond closely to the median values observed in the present study (Figure 9.25). Flemish medians are, however, consistently lower than those in the Boston and Denver study (Roche et al., 1979) and lower than the US reference values (Roberts & Maurer, 1977). Diastolic blood pressures are generally somewhat higher in Flemish girls than for the US sample reported by Roche et al. (1979) and Woynarowska et al. (1985). If we consider a systolic blood pressure of 140 mmHg and more and a diastolic

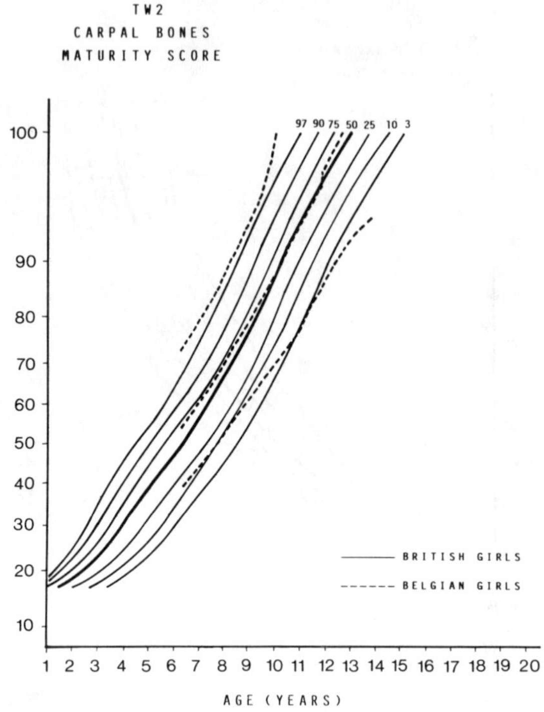

Figure 9.23. Percentile distribution of Flemish girls 6.0 to 18.0 years of age by CARP scores (TWII) compared to the distribution of British girls (GB). See note to Figure 9.22.

blood pressure of 90 mmHg and more as a risk factor for cardiovascular disease in children, then 0% of the girls are at risk for systolic blood pressure, but 3% to 5% are at risk for diastolic blood pressure. It can be questioned if these values, 140 mmHg and 90 mmHg, are indeed the exact cut-off points in children. As demonstrated by Woynarowska et al. (1985), children with higher blood pressure levels before puberty and with rapid increase during pubescence may have an increased risk of becoming hypertensive.

The medians for PWC170 in Flemish and Canadian girls (CAHPER, 1968) are nearly identical from 6 to 15.5 years. Thereafter, Canadian girls tend to taper off in their performance capacities whereas Flemish girls further increase their capacity from 430 kgm per minute to about 595 kgm per minute (Figure 9.26). In his study on worldwide variation in physiological work capacity, Shephard (1978, p. 208) also came to the conclusion that Europeans tend to outperform North Americans in physical work capacity.

The motor performance capacities of Flemish girls are compared to those reported by Bovend'eerdt et al. (1980) for a sample of Dutch girls and to those of North American girls (AAHPER, 1976; CAHPER, 1980; Branta et al. 1984; Haubenstricker & Seefeldt, 1986). The median values for arm pull of Dutch girls

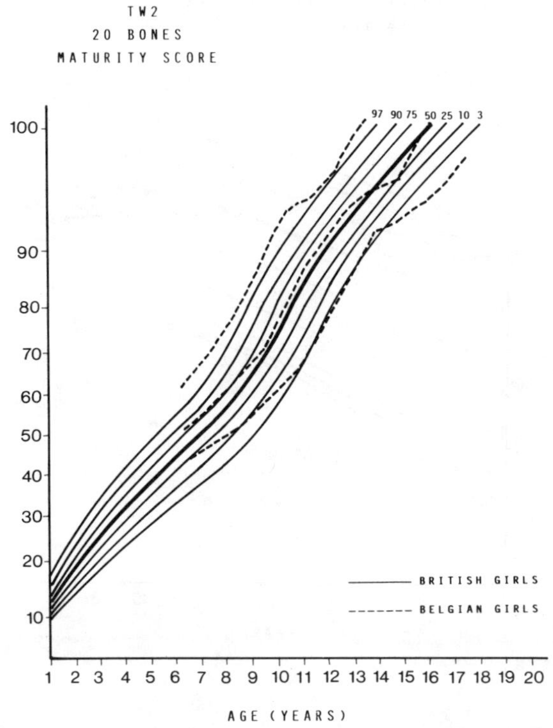

Figure 9.24. Percentile distribution of Flemish girls 6.0 to 18.0 years of age by 20-bone scores (TWII) compared to the distribution of British girls (GB). See note to Figure 9.22.

(Bovend'eerdt et al., 1980) coincide nearly exactly with those of Flemish girls between 12 and 18 years. It should be noted that the testing procedures were exactly the same; moreover, Bovend'eerdt came to our laboratory to familiarize himself with our testing procedures. Contrary to the similarities in static strength (arm pull) between Flemish and Dutch girls, quite large discrepancies are observed for explosive strength (vertical jump). The Dutch medians correspond to the P75 values between 12 and 17 years. Similarly the US values correspond at 6 years but shift to the P75 values at older ages (see Figure 9.27).

Still another trend in population differences is seen for trunk strength (leg lifts). Between 12 and 14 years the medians of Flemish and Dutch girls correspond closely, but thereafter the performance capacity decreases in Dutch girls whereas it further increases somewhat in Flemish girls. The functional strength (bent arm hang) of American girls is very similar to that of Flemish girls (Figure 9.28) but is much poorer than that of Dutch girls. This could be attributed to a difference in weight, since it is known that bent arm hang results are negatively influenced by weight at each age level. But Dutch girls, even in the sample studied by Bovend'eerdt et al. (1980), tend to be larger and heavier at each age level,

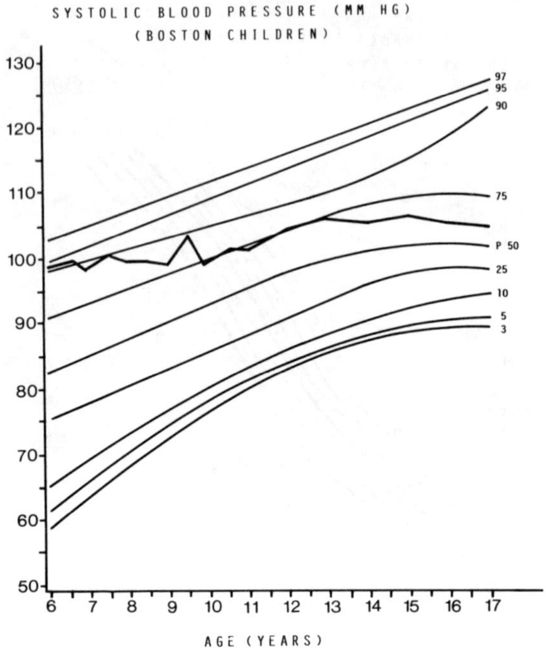

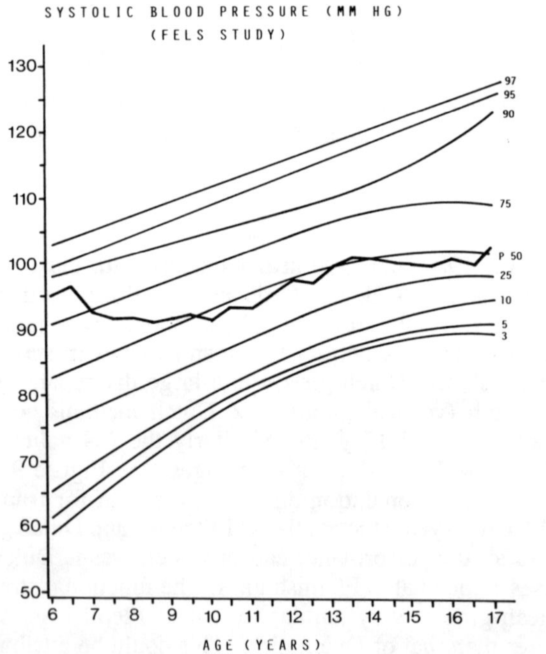

(Cont.)

Figure 9.25. Percentile distribution of Flemish girls 6.0 to 18.0 years of age by systolic blood pressure compared to medians from Boston children, the Fels study, and Denver children (Redrawn from Roche et al., 1979).

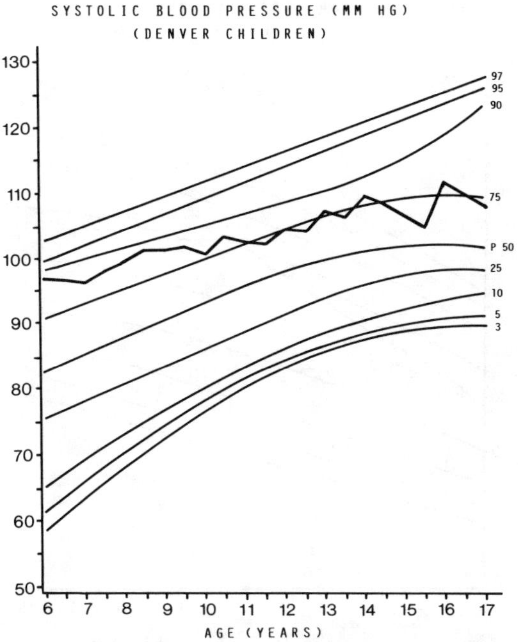

Figure 9.25. (Continued)

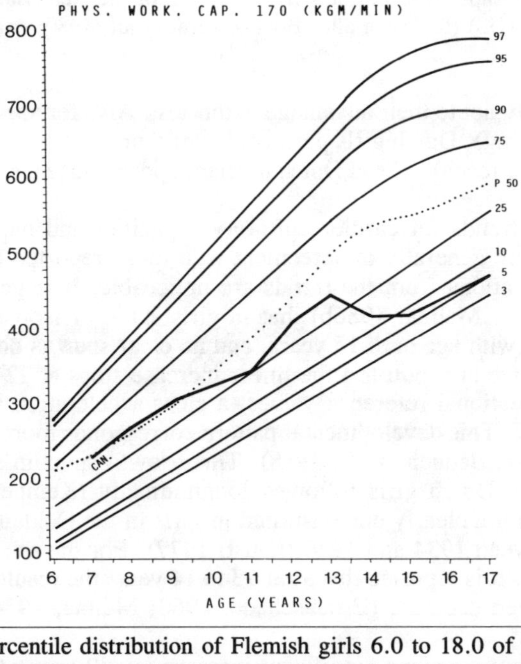

Figure 9.26. Percentile distribution of Flemish girls 6.0 to 18.0 of age by PWC170 compared to medians from a national sample of Canada (CAN) (Redrawn after CAHPER, 1968).

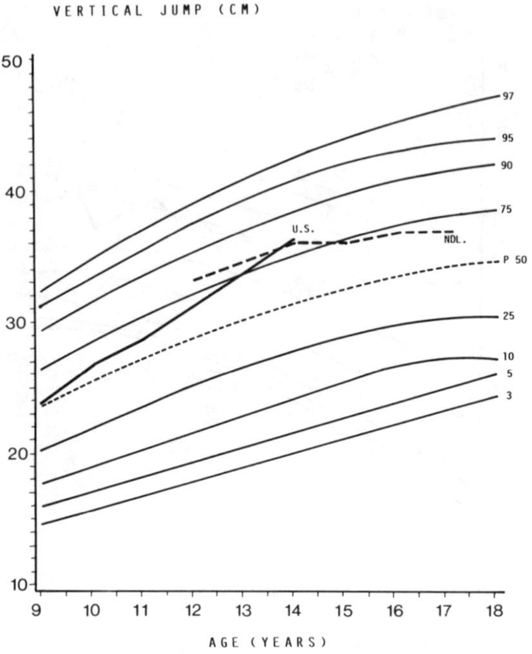

Figure 9.27. Percentile distribution of Flemish girls 6.0 to 18.0 years of age by vertical jump as compared to medians from samples of the Netherlands (NDL) and the United States (US) (Redrawn after Bovend'eerdt et al., 1980; Branta et al., 1984).

which is certainly not to their advantage in this test. Also for speed of limb movement (plate tapping), Dutch girls perform better than Flemish girls, whereas for flexibility (sit and reach) US and Dutch medians approximate the Flemish medians (Figure 9.29).

The major trends for cardiorespiratory capacities and motor performance characteristics are generally in agreement with those reported by others. However, some deviations from the trends are noticeable. It is generally reported (Asmussen, 1973; Malina, 1986b) that in girls static or isometric strength increases linearly with age until 15 years, and no clear spurt is observable. In our sample and for the arm pull test the linear increase stops at 12 years and, even in these cross-sectional reference values, a clear acceleration is seen followed by a tapering off. This developmental pattern corresponds more with the pattern observed in boys (Beunen et al., 1988). This growth spurt in static strength is also observed in Dutch girls followed longitudinally (Kemper & Verschuur, 1985a), but was not clearly demonstrated in girls in the Oakland Growth Study carried out between 1934 and 1946 (Faust, 1977). For the other motor performance capacities it is reported that after 13 to 14 years the results level off, form a plateau, or even decrease (Espenschade, 1960; Malina, 1974; Branta et al., 1984).

In the present sample a significant increase is still seen after 14 years for

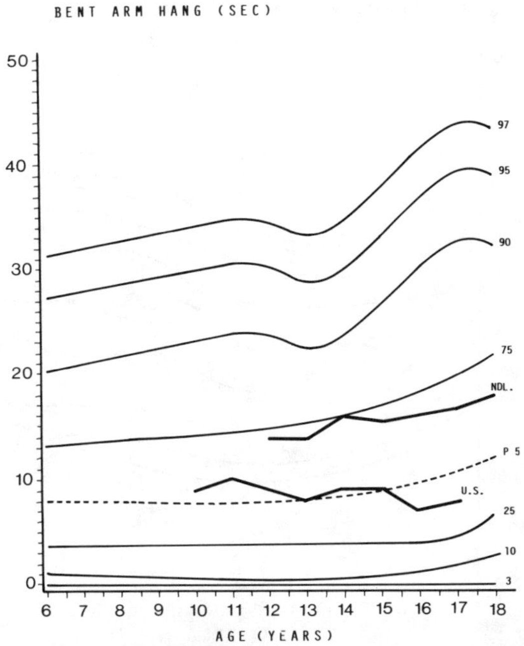

Figure 9.28. Percentile distribution of Flemish girls 6.0 to 18.0 years of age by bent arm hang as compared to medians from samples of the Netherlands (NDL) and the United States (US) (Redrawn after Bovend'eerdt et al., 1980; AAHPER, 1976).

vertical jump, leg lifts, bent arm hang, and plate tapping; a small increase in shuttle run results is also observable. In their overview of the most recent reports on motor performance, Haubenstricker and Seefeldt (1986) also noted a shift of the plateau toward slightly older ages. From the most recent studies of motor performance capacities in girls, it becomes apparent that the developmental patterns correspond more to those in boys, although large differences still became apparent between boys and girls, starting at puberty. This change in developmental pattern in motor performance can probably be explained by a changing lifestyle in adolescent girls.

No recent data on secular changes in physical activity patterns, lifestyle, eating habits, and performance capacities for Belgian girls are available. Inferences from other sources can, however, be made. Recently a trend toward a lower weight for height was observed in Belgian girls from 13 years onward (Vercauteren, Susanne, & Orban, 1984). This trend could be a reflection of the more active lifestyle of present-day adolescent girls and of their awareness that a more healthy lifestyle will keep their weight down. The hypothesis that contemporary adolescent girls are more active is confirmed by the findings on sport participation reported in chapter 12. Between 13.0 and 18.0 years, the total amount of sports participation of Flemish girls increased, which is in contrast to what had been reported previously.

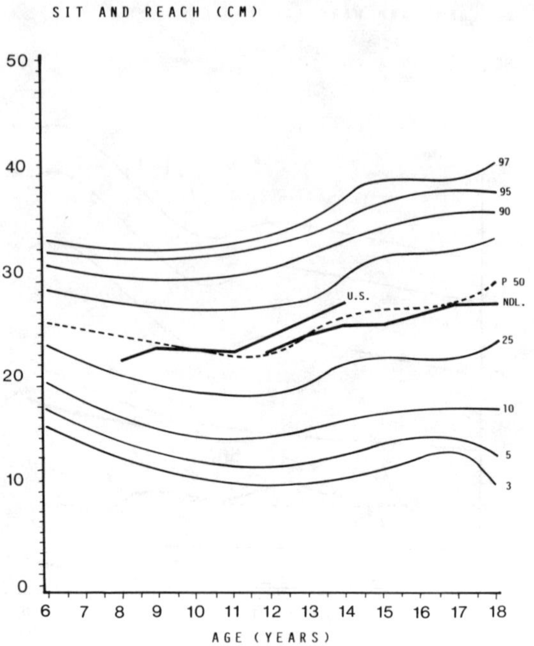

Figure 9.29. Percentile distribution of Flemish girls 6.0 to 18.0 years of age by sit and reach as compared to medians from samples of the Netherlands (NDL) and the United States (US). See note to Figure 9.27.

Chapter 10

The Age at Menarche

Rita Wellens and Robert M. Malina

Menarche, the first occurrence of menstruation, is a landmark in the sexual maturation process of the adolescent female. Although menarche is a biological process, it does not occur in a social vacuum. Rather, it has considerable significance in the psychological and emotional development of young girls. The age at menarche provides a good indicator of timing of sexual maturation, which can be used as a point of reference in analyses of growth and performance. At the level of the population, the average age at menarche is often used as an indicator of health and nutritional status, fecundity, and social conditions. In some countries, data on age at menarche have been collected over the past 100 to 150 years, thus providing a basis for examining secular changes in this developmental event.

The age at menarche in Flemish girls is considered subsequently. Descriptive statistics for the Leuven Growth Study of Flemish Girls are presented. Then comparisons of contemporary Belgian and European samples, and of secular changes in Flemish girls follow.

Procedures

During the anthropometric phase of the Leuven Growth Study of Flemish Girls, all girls in the fourth and subsequent grades were interviewed about menarcheal status (status quo method), and for the age at menarche if it had already occurred (retrospective method). In the former, the girls were simply asked to indicate if menarche had or had not occurred. For girls who had already attained menarche, each was asked to recall the time of the event as precisely as possible. When the student mentioned only month and year, the 15th of the month was noted next to the year of occurrence. When two months were mentioned, the first day of the second month was noted. When three months were mentioned, the 15th day of the second month was noted. For students who could recall only year and season, the middle of the season (day and month) was used to complement the information. The age at menarche was computed from the recalled dates and expressed in years and tenths.

Descriptive statistics for the status quo data were calculated with probit analysis (Finney, 1952), while those for the retrospective data were calculated with SAS procedures (SAS Institute, 1982). The 10th and 90th percentiles were also calculated for each set of data (Wellens, 1984).

Results

Status Quo Method

The status quo method is generally considered the best procedure for estimating the median age at menarche for a population. The total number of girls in each age group and the number and percentage who attained menarche in each age group in the Leuven Growth Study of Flemish Girls are given in Table 10.1.

Table 10.1 Status Quo Information for the Leuven Growth Study of Flemish Girls

Age group		Attained menarche	
(midpoint)	*n*	*f*	%
10.5	129	2	1.5
11.0	216	11	5.0
11.5	293	21	7.8
12.0	297	43	14.5
12.5	342	99	28.9
13.0	448	192	42.9
13.5	378	224	59.3
14.0	434	343	79.0
14.5	427	364	85.2
15.0	373	343	92.0
15.5	379	367	96.8
16.0	331	322	97.3
16.5	441	438	99.3
17.0	406	404	99.5
17.5	—	—	100.0

The median age at menarche is 13.20 + 0.02 years with a standard deviation of 1.25 years. The 10th and 90th percentiles are 11.58 and 14.82 years, respectively. Thus, 80% of the Flemish girls attain menarche between about 11.5 and 15.0 years of age.

Retrospective Method

Although the retrospective method is limited by error of recall, it is often used in longitudinal growth studies and in studies of special samples such as children with clinical problems and elite athletes. Recalled ages at menarche range from 7.56 to 17.03 years, with a mean age at menarche of 12.91 + 0.02 years and a standard deviation of 1.25 years. The median age at menarche is 12.94 years, and the 10th and 90th percentiles are 11.31 and 14.48 years, respectively (Wellens, 1984).

Descriptive statistics for the status quo and retrospective data are summarized in Table 10.2. The median age at menarche with the retrospective method is 0.26 years earlier than that with the status quo method. Corresponding differences between the 10th and 90th percentiles for each method are 0.27 and 0.34 years, respectively.

Table 10.2 Descriptive Statistics for Menarcheal Age (Years) With the Status Quo and Retrospective Methods in the Leuven Growth Study of Flemish Girls

	Status quo	Retrospective
Median	13.20	12.94
Mean	—	12.91
Standard deviation	1.25	1.25
Standard error	0.02	0.02
10th percentile	11.58	11.31
90th percentile	14.82	14.48
Range	—	7.56-17.03

Discussion

Status Quo and Retrospective Estimates

The differences between the 10th, 50th (median), and 90th percentiles for the status quo and retrospective estimates of the age at menarche are consistent with the observations of Bergsten-Brucefors (1976), who compared ages at menarche recorded during a longitudinal study with recalled ages at menarche about 4 years after the event. About two-thirds of the girls recalled the date of menarche within about three months. On the other hand, Beckers and Pleysier (1982b) reported no difference between ages at menarche with both methods in Belgian girls, a median of 12.9 years with the status quo method and a mean of 12.9 years with the retrospective method. Within subsamples of Flemish- and French-speaking girls, differences between median and mean ages at menarche were only about 0.1 year. Similar results were also reported for Swedish girls (Lindgren, 1976).

Mean ages at menarche, obtained with a "diary method" and the retrospective method, were identical.

Recent Estimates in European Girls

Median ages at menarche from recent surveys of Belgian girls and girls from several northwestern European countries are summarized in Table 10.3. The median age at menarche in the Leuven Growth Study of Flemish girls (13.2 years) (Wellens, 1984) is similar to that of an independent national sample of Flemish-speaking girls (13.1 years) (Beckers & Pleysier, 1982b), a sample of school girls

Table 10.3 Median/Mean Ages at Menarche and Standard Deviations for Samples of Northwestern European Girls Based on Surveys Done in the 1970s and 1980s

Country	*N*	Median/mean	*SD*
Belgium			
Leuven Growth Study of Flemish Girls	4,894	13.20	1.25
National	39,826	12.91	
Flemish-speaking	22,547	13.08	
French-speaking	17,279	12.83	
Brussels	1,048	13.06	
Netherlands			
National	3,067	13.28	
Utrecht	577	13.37	1.17
France			
Paris	40	12.92	0.71
rural	254	13.05	1.42
United Kingdom			
Northumberland	1,307	13.31	
Newcastle-Upon-Tyne	699	13.37	1.14
Federal Republic of Germany			
Bremerhaven	2,793	13.30	1.19
Mainz-Bingen	511	13.08	
Sweden			
Umea	88	13.11	0.99
urban	335	13.05	1.03
Norway			
Oslo	7,155	13.24	1.04

Note. Values are based on probit or logit estimates, or on empirical medians or means based on prospective data, except for the Swedish urban data, which are based upon combined "diary" and retrospective methods. References for the Belgian surveys are indicated in the text. All others are extracted from Danker-Hopfe (1986).

in Brussels (13.1 years) (Vercauteren & Susanne, 1984), and a national sample of Dutch girls (13.3 years).

In contrast, menarche is later than that for a national sample of French-speaking Belgian girls (12.8 years) (Beckers & Pleysier, 1982b). It should be noted that about 17% of the French-speaking sample of Beckers and Pleysier (1982b) were of foreign ancestry, that is, immigrant children from southern Europe and Africa, who were enrolled in the French-speaking schools. Only 2% of the Flemish-speaking sample were of foreign ancestry. The difference in the proportion of foreign children in the French and Flemish samples may be a contributory factor to the earlier median age at menarche in the French-speaking sample, since girls from southern Europe tend to attain menarche earlier than those in northern and northwestern Europe (Danker-Hopfe, 1986). On the other hand, the median age at menarche for French-speaking girls in Belgium is quite similar to that for a small prospective sample of Parisian girls (12.9 years, Table 10.3). The median age at menarche for Flemish girls thus falls well within the range of medians/means from recent surveys in northwestern Europe. Median and/or mean ages at menarche range from 12.8 and 12.9 years in French-speaking Belgian and Parisian girls, respectively, to 13.4 years in girls from Utrecht in The Netherlands and Newcastle-Upon-Tyne in the United Kingdom (Table 10.3). Standard deviations are also similar in most of the surveys that report them.

Secular Comparisons in Belgium

Menarcheal information from several surveys in Belgium permit an estimate of secular changes in this developmental event. Jeurissen (1969) reported a survey of menarche in 15,419 Belgian girls in Limburg and Brabant born between 1915 and 1959. The sample was comprised of (a) sisters of patients who were hospitalized for tuberculosis in either the foundation Baronne Lucie Lambert in Limburg or dispensaries in Brabant, (b) family members of the personnel at these institutions, and (c) family members of children who tested positive for tuberculosis at these institutions. The data include status quo menarcheal information for 15,419 girls 9 through 18 years of age. These data are apparently from the hospital/dispensary records. In addition, retrospective information was gathered for 1,289 girls and women born between 1915 and 1949.

The status quo data were analyzed using cumulative percentages to derive percentile distributions by birth year cohorts, including, of course, medians. Knops and Van Landeghem (1969) surveyed 2,494 school girls in Leuven in 1964 and 1965, while Vercauteren and Susanne (1984) surveyed 1,048 school girls in Brussels in 1980. In the latter survey, the authors compared results of a probit analysis with those based on the analytic procedures of Jeurissen (1969). The difference between medians was 0.06 year. In addition to these regional surveys, Beckers and Pleysier (1982b) reported the results of a national survey of Belgian school girls. The 1980-1981 survey was based on a stratified national sample of about 40,000 girls and included information on type of school and language spoken. Only the results for Flemish-speaking girls are used in the evaluation of secular changes.

Median ages at menarche and the 10th and 90th percentiles for Belgian women and girls grouped by year of birth are illustrated in Figure 10.1. It appears that the median age at menarche in Belgium was fairly stable at about 14.4 years among

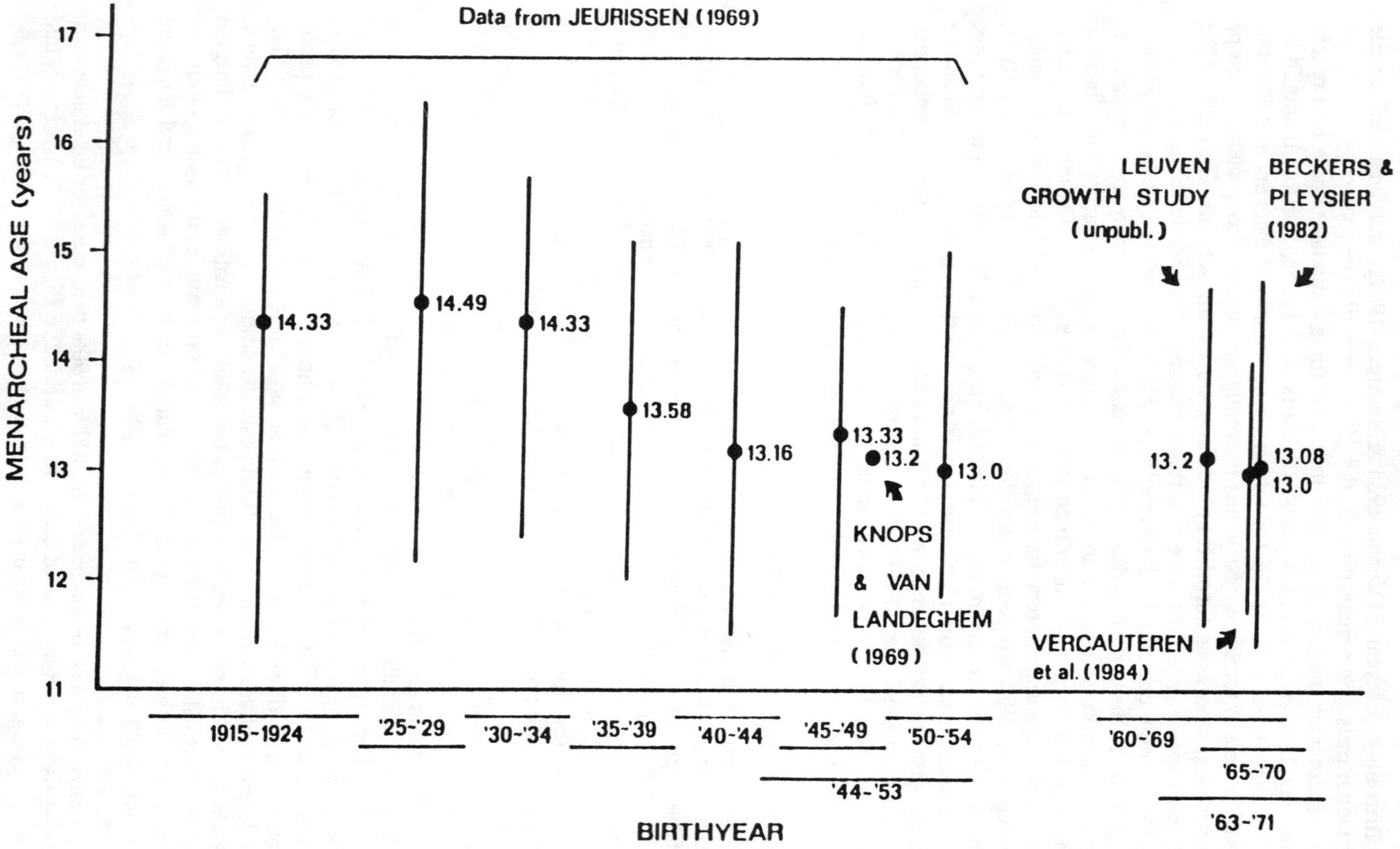

Figure 10.1. Median ages at menarche and the 10th and 90th percentiles in Flemish girls grouped by year of birth.

women born between 1915 and 1934. However, the age at which 10% of the women attained menarche, that is, the 10th percentile, increased by about one year over this time, while the age at which 90% of the women attained menarche increased by almost one year in women born between 1915 to 1924 and 1925 to 1929, and then declined to the earlier level in women born between 1930 to 1934. The women born between 1925 and 1929, of course, would have attained menarche during World War II. Median age at menarche then declined to 13.6 and 13.2 years in women born just before and during World War II, between 1935 to 1939 and 1940 to 1944, respectively.

Subsequently, there appeared to be a slight rise in the median age at menarche to 13.3 years among those born after World War II, 1945 to 1949. Median ages at menarche derived from status quo surveys of Belgian girls born between 1943 and 1971 are reasonably stable between 13.0 and 13.2 years. Thus, it would appear that the secular decline in the median age at menarche in Flemish women occurred after World War II (i.e., women born before and during the war), and that the trend has stopped since the mid-1950s. The same trend is also apparent for the 10th percentiles of the distributions of menarcheal ages. The age at which 10% of Flemish women attain menarche has been fairly stable since the 1950s, varying between 11.5 and 11.8 years. On the other hand, the 95th percentiles of the distributions of menarcheal ages have been more variable during this time. They fluctuate between 14.0 to 15.1 years.

Chapter 11

Norm Scales and Profile Charts for Anthropometric Measurements, Motor Fitness, Physiological Measurements, and Skeletal Maturity

Johan Lefevre

Norm Scales

If a raw score is the only information available about an anthropometric or physiological measurement or about the test performance or maturity of a girl, interpretation of the score is difficult. Additional interpretative data is needed, therefore the raw scores are transformed into derived scores before direct comparisons are made. Derived scores are expressed in one of two major ways:

1. Developmental level attained (to indicate how far along the normal path the individual has progressed). Such a way of working produces age norms, and

2. Relative position within a specified group—With such norms, the individual's somatic, physiological, motor, or maturity score is evaluated in terms of the score of the most nearly comparable standardization group; namely, with the score of children of the same chronological age group. Within-group norms are derived scores that are determined from the raw scores obtained by a specific group on a specific test. They are established by determining how a representative group of persons actually performs in a test. Any individual's raw score is then referred to the distribution of scores obtained by the standardization sample to discover where he or she falls in that distribution.

It was decided to use percentile norms for this study. A percentile indicates the individual's relative position in the standardization sample. It is expressed in terms of the percentage of persons in the standardization sample who fall below a given raw score. A 12-year-old girl who obtains a raw score of 43 kg on the weight measurement (see Table 11.1) has a derived percentile score of P59. This means that 59% of the girls between 12.0 and 12.5 years of age have a lower weight score than this particular girl. In the growth curves the most important percentile points were included and their evolution was described according to age. Only the most commonly used percentiles were included to assess the normality of growth and development of the measurements and tests under consideration.

In Tables 11.1 to 11.4, percentiles corresponding to the observed raw scores for weight, height, arm pull, and sit and reach are given for girls between 6.0 and 18.5 years of age.[1] For ease of use, these tables are so constructed that in the first column the raw scores (value) are given, and in the subsequent columns the corresponding percentile scores are recorded separately for each age level. For the growth curves, the age groupings have been divided into half-yearly intervals. Since the total range in the inter-individual variability between 6.0 and 18.5 years of age had to be covered in most tables, it is evident that for a given age level a given raw score may fall outside the total percentile range. In this case a dot has been printed. This method of presenting the percentile scores has the further advantage that the shift between ages in the measurements and performances is clearly demonstrated. As does Safrit (1973, p. 243), we would like to stress that no inherent value is attached to any given norm score. The norm identifies a person in relation to a given population. Therefore, the final evaluation and interpretation of an individual score is made by the person using the norm scale.

Profile Charts

If we wish to compare a girl's score on one measurement or test with her score on another measurement or test, the direct comparison of raw scores would be meaningless. Therefore, the raw scores should be transformed into relative scores before direct comparisons can be made. From these relative scores, profile charts can be constructed. These profile charts are useful diagnostic tools to obtain a quick view of the somatic or physiological characteristics or of the general motor ability of a single girl. The result in one measurement or test can easily be compared with those in other measurements or tests.

The profile charts are constructed for each age group on the basis of the norm scales. Only the age group 12.0 to 12.5 years has been shown.[2] Age groups have been divided into half-yearly intervals. The raw scores for each measurement and test were located on a chart together with the corresponding percentiles (see Tables 11.5 and 11.6). The vertical column in the middle of the chart indicates the P50 values. To the left of this, the P25, P10, and P3 values are located, and to the right, the P75, P90, and P97 values. This means that for all values to the right of P50, less than 50% of the standardizing sample obtained results "higher" or "better" than this score, whereas for all values to the left of P50, more than 50% of the standardizing sample scored "higher" or "better." Taking into account their respective percentages, the same holds true for the raw scores located above or below the P3, P10, P25, P75, P90, and P97 columns. These percentile scores can be divided into eight classes for each measurement or test separately. Schematically, the following interpretation can be given for the motor tests.

Class	*Percentile score*	*Evaluation*
1	< = P3	extremely weak
2	P3-P10	very weak
3	P10-P25	weak
4	P25-P50	on the average weak
5	P50-P75	on the average good
6	P75-P90	good
7	P90-P97	very good
8	> = P97	extremely good

By means of this profile, it is easy to detect in which test(s) the individual girl is classified as "good," "on the average," or "weak" with respect to girls of the same chronological age group. Separate profiles are given for half-year age groupings for the anthropometric measurements (Table 11.5), for the motor ability tests and for the physiological measurements (Table 11.6). The following procedure can be used to draw up an individual profile: (a) Take the profile chart of the age group to which a girl belongs, (b) locate in the left column the measurement or test against which the individual score is to be assessed, and (c) indicate the score of the girl in the right place, which will show in which percentile class the girl is situated.

The different individual scores can be plotted and the points connected. This profile gives an overall picture of the body structure, the motor ability, and/or the physiological capacity of a girl in relation to her age group. Individual interpretations can be made; however, in interpreting the results one must take into account that each measurement or test result is affected by a measurement error. Therefore small differences in the location of test results should be ignored. It should also be remembered that, for body dimensions especially, the different dimensions are to some extent interrelated. This means that a girl who is tall for her age, say located between P75 and P90, is also likely to be fairly heavy unless she is of a very linear build, in which case she would score rather low on bone width dimensions such as biacromial diameter, chest width, bicristal diameter, bicondylar femur, and bicondylar humerus. In this case she would also obtain rather small values for most circumferences and skinfolds.

Bearing in mind that the motor test battery has been constructed on the basis of factor analyses so that each test measures a separate factor, very low correlations have been found between the oblique factors (see Table 1.4 in chapter 1). Consequently the interrelationship between the motor tests is low. This means that the result in one test does not affect the result in another. Moreover, most motor tests bear little relation to body dimensions. Only for static strength (arm pull) are there fairly high positive correlations with several body dimensions, especially weight and height. For functional strength (bent arm hang) and, to a lesser extent, for trunk strength (leg lifts), negative correlations are found with weight and height. It is often advisable to consider body dimensions in evaluating individual results, especially for obese or slender girls. For all these reasons, a better result in static strength (arm pull) and fairly low scores in functional strength (bent arm hang) are to be expected for obese girls and vice versa for slender girls.

Table 11.1a Percentile Scores for Weight (kg) by Age (6 to 12 Years)

AGE	6.0 6.5	6.5 7.0	7.0 7.5	7.5 8.0	8.0 8.5	8.5 9.0
VALUE						
17	3	1	.	.	.	.
18	9	5	2	0	.	.
19	18	11	7	3	1	.
20	30	22	14	7	4	1
21	44	34	24	15	8	4
22	59	48	36	24	15	8
23	75	61	49	36	24	14
24	80	74	61	48	35	22
25	86	80	72	59	46	32
26	92	86	79	68	56	42
27	98	91	85	77	64	52
28	.	95	90	83	73	60
29	.	98	93	88	79	68
30	.	.	95	91	84	75
31	.	.	96	94	89	80
32	.	.	98	95	92	85
33	.	.	.	96	93	89
34	.	.	.	97	95	91
35	.	.	.	98	96	93
36	.	.	.	.	96	94
37	.	.	.	.	97	95
38	.	.	.	.	98	96
39	.	.	.	.	.	97
40	.	.	.	.	.	97
41	.	.	.	.	.	.
42	.	.	.	.	.	.
43	.	.	.	.	.	.
44	.	.	.	.	.	.
45	.	.	.	.	.	.
46	.	.	.	.	.	.
47	.	.	.	.	.	.
48	.	.	.	.	.	.
49	.	.	.	.	.	.
50	.	.	.	.	.	.
51	.	.	.	.	.	.
52	.	.	.	.	.	.
53	.	.	.	.	.	.
54	.	.	.	.	.	.
55	.	.	.	.	.	.
56	.	.	.	.	.	.
57	.	.	.	.	.	.
58	.	.	.	.	.	.
59	.	.	.	.	.	.
60	.	.	.	.	.	.

9.0	9.5	10.0	10.5	11.0	11.5	12.0
9.5	10.0	10.5	11.0	11.5	12.0	12.5
.	.	.	.	.	.	.
.	.	.	.	.	.	.
.	.	.	.	.	.	.
.	.	.	.	.	.	.
2	.	.	.	.	.	.
4	1	.	.	.	.	.
7	3	1	.	.	.	.
13	6	3	.	.	.	.
20	11	5	2	.	.	.
28	17	9	4	2	.	.
38	24	14	7	3	.	.
47	32	20	11	6	3	.
55	41	27	17	9	4	2
62	50	35	22	13	7	3
69	56	43	29	18	10	5
76	63	51	36	23	14	8
80	69	57	43	29	19	10
84	75	63	50	36	23	15
88	79	68	56	43	29	19
91	82	74	61	49	35	23
92	86	78	67	55	41	28
93	89	81	72	60	47	33
95	91	83	76	65	53	39
95	92	86	79	70	57	45
96	93	89	81	75	62	50
97	94	91	84	77	67	55
97	95	92	86	79	72	59
.	96	93	89	81	76	63
.	97	94	90	84	78	68
.	98	95	92	86	80	72
.	.	96	93	88	82	76
.	.	97	94	90	84	78
.	.	98	95	91	86	80
.	.	.	96	92	88	82
.	.	.	97	94	90	84
.	.	.	.	95	91	86
.	.	.	.	96	92	88
.	.	.	.	98	94	90
.	.	.	.	.	95	92
.	.	.	.	.	96	93
.	.	.	.	.	98	94
.	.	.	.	.	.	95
.	.	.	.	.	.	96
.	.	.	.	.	.	97

Table 11.1b Percentile Scores for Weight (kg) by Age (12.5 to 18 Years)

AGE VALUE	12.5 13.0	13.0 13.5	13.5 14.0	14.0 14.5	14.5 15.0	15.0 15.5
31	2	.	.	.	.	.
32	4	.	.	.	.	.
33	6	2	.	.	.	.
34	8	4	.	.	.	.
35	11	6	3	.	.	.
36	14	8	4	.	.	.
37	18	11	6	3	.	.
38	22	14	8	4	.	.
39	26	17	10	5	3	.
40	31	21	13	7	4	2
41	36	24	16	9	5	3
42	42	29	20	12	7	4
43	47	34	23	16	9	5
44	52	38	26	19	13	8
45	56	43	31	22	16	11
46	60	48	36	25	20	15
47	64	52	41	31	24	19
48	68	56	45	36	29	24
49	72	61	50	41	34	29
50	76	65	55	47	40	34
51	78	69	59	52	45	40
52	80	73	64	57	51	45
53	83	76	69	61	55	50
54	85	79	73	66	60	55
55	87	81	77	71	65	60
56	89	84	79	75	69	64
57	91	86	82	78	74	69
58	92	89	84	80	77	74
59	93	91	86	83	79	77
60	94	92	89	85	82	79
61	95	93	91	87	84	81
62	96	94	92	90	86	84
63	97	95	93	91	89	86
64	97	96	94	92	91	88
65	.	96	95	93	92	90
66	.	97	95	94	93	91
67	.	97	96	95	94	92
68	.	.	96	96	95	93
69	.	.	97	96	95	94
70	.	.	97	96	96	95
71	.	.	.	97	96	96
72	.	.	.	97	97	96
73	.	.	.	.	97	97
74	.	.	.	.	.	97
75	.	.	.	.	.	.
76	.	.	.	.	.	.
77	.	.	.	.	.	.

15.5–16.0	16.0–16.5	16.5–17.0	17.0–17.5	17.5–18.0	18.0–18.5
.	.	.	.	.	.
.	.	.	.	.	.
.	.	.	.	.	.
.	.	.	.	.	.
.	.	.	.	.	.
.	.	.	.	.	.
.	.	.	.	.	.
.	.	.	.	.	.
.	.	.	.	.	.
.	.	.	.	.	.
.	.	.	.	.	.
3	.	.	.	.	.
4	3	1	.	.	.
5	4	3	2	2	2
8	6	5	5	4	4
11	9	8	7	6	5
16	13	10	9	8	7
20	17	14	12	10	9
24	21	18	16	14	12
29	25	22	20	18	16
35	30	26	24	22	20
40	36	32	29	26	24
45	41	37	34	32	29
51	47	43	40	38	36
55	52	49	46	43	42
60	56	54	51	49	48
65	61	58	56	54	53
69	66	63	61	59	59
74	70	68	66	64	64
77	75	72	70	69	69
79	77	76	75	74	74
82	80	79	78	78	77
84	82	81	81	80	79
86	85	84	83	83	82
89	87	86	86	86	84
90	90	89	89	89	86
91	91	91	90	91	89
92	92	91	91	91	90
93	93	92	92	92	91
94	94	93	93	93	92
95	95	94	94	94	93
96	96	95	95	95	94
97	96	96	96	96	95
97	97	97	97	96	96
.	.	98	97	97	96
.	.	.	.	98	97
.	.	.	.	.	97

Table 11.2a Percentile Scores for Height (cm) by Age (6 to 12 Years)

AGE	6.0 6.5	6.5 7.0	7.0 7.5	7.5 8.0	8.0 8.5	8.5 9.0
VALUE						
107	2	.	.	.	.	.
108	4	.	.	.	.	.
109	6	.	.	.	.	.
110	8	3	.	.	.	.
111	12	5	.	.	.	.
112	17	7	2	.	.	.
113	22	9	4	.	.	.
114	29	14	6	.	.	.
115	36	19	8	3	.	.
116	44	24	11	4	.	.
117	52	31	16	7	2	.
118	60	38	20	9	4	.
119	69	45	25	13	5	.
120	77	53	32	17	8	3
121	84	61	40	22	10	4
122	90	69	47	27	14	6
123	92	77	54	34	19	9
124	94	83	62	41	23	11
125	96	89	69	48	29	16
126	98	91	76	55	36	20
127	.	93	82	62	42	24
128	.	95	87	70	49	31
129	.	97	91	76	56	37
130	.	99	93	81	63	43
131	.	.	95	86	70	50
132	.	.	96	90	76	57
133	.	.	98	92	80	63
134	.	.	.	94	85	70
135	.	.	.	96	89	76
136	.	.	.	97	92	80
137	.	.	.	.	93	84
138	.	.	.	.	95	88
139	.	.	.	.	97	91
140	.	.	.	.	98	93
141	.	.	.	.	.	95
142	.	.	.	.	.	96
143	.	.	.	.	.	98
144	.	.	.	.	.	.
145	.	.	.	.	.	.
146	.	.	.	.	.	.
147	.	.	.	.	.	.
148	.	.	.	.	.	.
149	.	.	.	.	.	.
150	.	.	.	.	.	.
151	.	.	.	.	.	.
152	.	.	.	.	.	.
153	.	.	.	.	.	.
154	.	.	.	.	.	.
155	.	.	.	.	.	.
156	.	.	.	.	.	.
157	.	.	.	.	.	.
158	.	.	.	.	.	.
159	.	.	.	.	.	.
160	.	.	.	.	.	.
161	.	.	.	.	.	.
162	.	.	.	.	.	.
163	.	.	.	.	.	.
164	.	.	.	.	.	.
165	.	.	.	.	.	.

9.0 9.5	9.5 10.0	10.0 10.5	10.5 11.0	11.0 11.5	11.5 12.0	12.0 12.5
.	.	.	.	.	.	.
.	.	.	.	.	.	.
.	.	.	.	.	.	.
.	.	.	.	.	.	.
.	.	.	.	.	.	.
.	.	.	.	.	.	.
.	.	.	.	.	.	.
.	.	.	.	.	.	.
.	.	.	.	.	.	.
.	.	.	.	.	.	.
.	.	.	.	.	.	.
.	.	.	.	.	.	.
.	.	.	.	.	.	.
.	.	.	.	.	.	.
.	.	.	.	.	.	.
2	.	.	.	.	.	.
4	.	.	.	.	.	.
5	.	.	.	.	.	.
7	3	.	.	.	.	.
9	4	.	.	.	.	.
13	6	2	.	.	.	.
17	8	4	.	.	.	.
21	10	5	.	.	.	.
26	14	7	3	.	.	.
32	19	9	4	.	.	.
38	23	12	6	2	.	.
45	27	16	8	4	.	.
51	34	20	10	5	.	.
57	40	24	13	7	3	.
64	46	29	17	9	4	.
70	52	35	21	11	5	.
76	58	41	25	14	7	3
80	64	47	30	18	9	4
83	70	52	36	21	12	6
87	76	58	42	25	15	8
90	79	64	48	31	18	9
92	82	69	53	37	22	12
94	86	75	58	42	25	15
96	89	78	63	48	31	18
97	92	82	68	53	36	21
.	94	85	74	58	42	24
.	95	88	77	63	48	29
.	97	91	81	67	53	35
.	98	93	84	72	57	41
.	.	95	87	76	62	46
.	.	96	90	80	66	52
.	.	97	92	83	71	57
.	.	.	94	87	75	61
.	.	.	96	90	79	66
.	.	.	97	92	83	71
.	.	.	98	94	87	76
.	.	.	.	96	90	80
.	.	.	.	97	92	84
.	.	.	.	98	94	88
.	.	.	.	.	96	91
.	.	.	.	.	97	93
.	.	.	.	.	98	95
.	.	.	.	.	.	96
.	.	.	.	.	.	97

Table 11.2b Percentile Scores for Height (cm) by Age (12.5 to 18 Years)

AGE	12.5 13.0	13.0 13.5	13.5 14.0	14.0 14.5	14.5 15.0	15.0 15.5
VALUE						
141	3	.	.	.	.	.
142	4	.	.	.	.	.
143	6	.	.	.	.	.
144	7	3	.	.	.	.
145	9	4	.	.	.	.
146	12	6	2	.	.	.
147	15	8	4	.	.	.
148	18	9	5	3	.	.
149	21	12	7	4	2	.
150	24	15	9	6	4	3
151	29	19	11	7	5	4
152	35	22	15	9	7	5
153	40	26	18	12	9	7
154	46	32	22	16	11	9
155	51	37	26	19	14	11
156	57	43	31	23	18	15
157	63	49	37	28	22	18
158	68	55	43	34	26	22
159	74	61	49	40	33	27
160	78	67	55	46	39	33
161	82	73	62	52	45	40
162	86	78	68	59	52	47
163	90	82	75	65	58	53
164	92	86	79	72	64	59
165	95	90	83	77	70	65
166	96	92	87	81	76	71
167	97	94	91	85	80	76
168	98	96	93	89	84	80
169	.	97	95	92	88	84
170	.	98	96	94	91	88
171	.	.	97	96	93	91
172	.	.	.	97	95	93
173	.	.	.	98	96	95
174	.	.	.	.	98	97
175	.	.	.	.	.	98
176	.	.	.	.	.	.
177	.	.	.	.	.	.

15.5 16.0	16.0 16.5	16.5 17.0	17.0 17.5	17.5 18.0	18.0 18.5
.	.	.	.	.	.
.	.	.	.	.	.
.	.	.	.	.	.
.	.	.	.	.	.
.	.	.	.	.	.
.	.	.	.	.	.
.	.	.	.	.	.
.	.	.	.	.	.
.	.	.	.	.	.
2	.	.	.	.	.
3	2	2	.	.	.
4	4	3	2	.	.
6	5	4	4	3	.
7	7	6	5	4	3
9	8	8	7	6	5
12	10	10	9	8	7
16	14	13	12	11	9
20	18	17	16	15	14
24	22	21	20	20	19
29	27	25	25	25	25
36	34	32	31	31	31
43	41	39	38	37	37
50	47	46	45	44	43
56	54	52	51	50	49
61	59	58	57	56	55
67	65	63	62	62	61
73	70	69	68	67	67
78	76	74	73	73	73
82	80	79	78	78	77
86	84	83	83	82	81
90	88	88	87	86	84
92	91	91	91	90	88
94	93	93	93	93	91
96	95	95	95	95	93
97	97	97	97	96	95
.	.	.	.	97	96
.	.	.	.	.	97

Table 11.3a Percentile Scores for Arm Pull (kg) by Age (6 to 12 Years)

AGE	6.0 6.5	6.5 7.0	7.0 7.5	7.5 8.0	8.0 8.5	8.5 9.0
VALUE						
9	0	.	.	.	.	.
10	7	2	.	.	.	.
11	13	7	3	.	.	.
12	23	12	7	3	1	.
13	32	21	12	6	3	1
14	42	30	19	11	6	3
15	53	39	27	18	10	6
16	66	49	36	25	17	10
17	77	60	46	34	23	16
18	82	72	55	43	31	22
19	87	79	66	52	40	29
20	94	84	75	61	49	37
21	96	89	81	70	57	46
22	97	94	86	77	65	54
23	.	96	91	83	74	61
24	.	97	94	88	79	69
25	.	.	96	92	85	76
26	.	.	97	94	90	81
27	.	.	.	96	92	86
28	.	.	.	97	94	90
29	.	.	.	.	96	92
30	.	.	.	.	97	94
31	.	.	.	.	.	96
32	.	.	.	.	.	97
33	.	.	.	.	.	.
34	.	.	.	.	.	.
35	.	.	.	.	.	.
36	.	.	.	.	.	.
37	.	.	.	.	.	.
38	.	.	.	.	.	.
39	.	.	.	.	.	.
40	.	.	.	.	.	.
41	.	.	.	.	.	.
42	.	.	.	.	.	.
43	.	.	.	.	.	.
44	.	.	.	.	.	.
45	.	.	.	.	.	.
46	.	.	.	.	.	.

9.0 9.5	9.5 10.0	10.0 10.5	10.5 11.0	11.0 11.5	11.5 12.0	12.0 12.5
.	.	.	.	.	.	.
.	.	.	.	.	.	.
.	.	.	.	.	.	.
.	.	.	.	.	.	.
.	.	.	.	.	.	.
1	.	.	.	.	.	.
3	2	.	.	.	.	.
6	4	2	.	.	.	.
10	6	4	2	.	.	.
15	9	6	4	2	.	.
21	14	9	6	4	3	.
27	20	14	9	6	4	3
35	25	19	13	9	6	4
43	33	24	18	13	9	6
51	41	31	23	17	12	9
58	48	38	29	22	17	12
65	55	46	36	27	21	16
72	62	53	43	34	25	20
78	68	59	50	41	32	24
83	75	65	56	48	39	30
88	79	71	62	54	46	37
91	84	76	68	59	52	43
93	89	81	73	65	57	50
94	91	85	78	70	62	55
96	93	89	82	75	67	60
97	94	91	86	79	72	65
.	96	93	90	83	77	69
.	97	94	91	86	80	74
.	.	96	93	90	83	78
.	.	97	94	92	87	81
.	.	.	96	93	90	84
.	.	.	97	94	92	87
.	.	.	.	96	93	90
.	.	.	.	97	94	91
.	.	.	.	.	96	93
.	.	.	.	.	97	94
.	.	.	.	.	.	96
.	.	.	.	.	.	97

Table 11.3b Percentile Scores for Arm Pull (kg) by Age (12.5 to 18 Years)

AGE	12.5 13.0	13.0 13.5	13.5 14.0	14.0 14.5	14.5 15.0	15.0 15.5
VALUE						
21	3	.	.	.	.	.
22	4	3	.	.	.	.
23	6	4	3	2	.	.
24	8	6	4	3	2	.
25	12	8	6	4	3	2
26	15	11	8	6	4	3
27	19	15	10	7	6	5
28	23	18	13	9	8	6
29	28	22	17	12	9	8
30	34	26	21	16	12	10
31	41	32	25	20	16	13
32	47	37	30	24	19	16
33	52	43	34	28	23	20
34	57	49	39	32	27	23
35	62	54	44	36	31	27
36	67	58	48	40	35	31
37	71	63	53	44	39	35
38	76	68	58	48	43	39
39	78	73	63	53	47	43
40	81	76	68	57	51	47
41	84	79	73	62	55	51
42	87	82	77	67	59	54
43	90	84	79	72	63	58
44	91	87	82	76	67	62
45	93	90	84	78	71	66
46	94	91	87	81	75	70
47	96	93	89	84	78	74
48	97	94	91	86	81	77
49	.	96	93	89	83	80
50	.	97	94	91	86	82
51	.	98	95	92	89	85
52	.	.	96	94	91	88
53	.	.	97	95	93	90
54	.	.	98	96	94	92
55	.	.	.	97	95	94
56	.	.	.	97	96	95
57	.	.	.	.	97	96
58	.	.	.	.	97	96
59	.	.	.	.	.	97
60	.	.	.	.	.	.
61	.	.	.	.	.	.

15.5 16.0	16.0 16.5	16.5 17.0	17.0 17.5	17.5 18.0	18.0 18.5
.	.	.	.	.	.
.	.	.	.	.	.
.	.	.	.	.	.
.	.	.	.	.	.
.	.	.	.	.	.
2	.	.	.	.	.
3	2	.	.	.	.
5	4	2	.	.	.
6	5	4	2	.	.
8	7	5	4	3	.
11	9	7	5	4	3
14	12	10	8	6	4
17	15	13	10	8	6
20	18	16	13	10	8
23	21	19	17	14	9
27	24	22	20	17	13
31	28	25	23	21	17
35	32	29	26	24	22
39	37	34	31	28	26
44	41	39	36	33	31
48	46	43	41	38	35
52	50	48	46	43	39
56	54	52	51	48	44
60	58	56	55	52	48
63	62	60	59	56	52
67	66	64	63	60	56
71	70	68	67	64	60
75	74	72	71	68	64
78	77	76	75	72	68
80	79	78	78	76	71
83	82	81	80	79	75
86	84	84	83	81	78
88	87	86	85	84	82
91	90	89	88	86	85
92	91	91	90	89	88
94	93	92	92	92	92
95	94	94	93	94	95
96	95	95	95	95	96
97	96	96	96	96	96
97	97	97	97	97	97
.	.	.	98	98	97

Table 11.4a Percentile Scores for Sit and Reach (cm) by Age (6 to 12 Years)

AGE	6.0 6.5	6.5 7.0	7.0 7.5	7.5 8.0	8.0 8.5	8.5 9.0
VALUE						
9	.	.	.	.	.	.
10	.	.	.	.	.	.
11	.	.	.	.	.	2
12	.	.	.	2	3	4
13	.	.	2	3	4	5
14	.	3	4	5	6	7
15	3	4	5	7	8	9
16	4	5	7	9	10	12
17	6	7	9	11	14	16
18	7	9	12	15	17	19
19	9	13	16	19	21	23
20	13	17	20	23	25	28
21	17	21	24	27	31	34
22	21	25	31	35	38	41
23	27	34	39	42	45	47
24	38	43	47	50	52	55
25	49	52	55	58	60	62
26	57	60	63	66	68	70
27	65	68	71	74	76	77
28	73	76	78	80	82	83
29	80	83	85	87	88	89
30	86	89	91	91	92	92
31	92	93	94	94	94	95
32	95	96	96	97	97	97
33	97	98	98	99	99	99
34	.	.	.	.	.	.

9.0 9.5	9.5 10.0	10.0 10.5	10.5 11.0	11.0 11.5	11.5 12.0	12.0 12.5
.	.	.	.	2	2	2
.	2	3	3	3	3	3
3	4	4	4	5	5	5
4	5	6	6	6	6	6
6	7	8	8	8	8	8
8	9	10	10	10	10	10
10	12	13	13	14	14	13
14	15	16	17	17	17	17
18	19	20	21	21	21	21
21	22	23	24	25	25	25
25	26	28	30	31	31	31
31	33	35	36	38	38	37
37	39	41	43	44	44	43
43	45	47	49	51	51	49
50	52	54	55	56	56	55
57	59	60	61	62	62	61
64	65	66	67	67	67	66
71	72	73	73	73	72	72
78	78	78	78	78	77	77
84	84	84	83	83	82	81
90	90	89	88	87	86	85
92	92	92	92	91	90	89
95	95	95	95	94	93	92
97	97	97	96	96	95	95
99	99	98	98	97	97	96
.	.	.	.	.	98	98

Table 11.4b Percentile Scores for Sit and Reach (cm) by Age (12.5 to 18 Years)

AGE	12.5 13.0	13.0 13.5	13.5 14.0	14.0 14.5	14.5 15.0	15.0 15.5
VALUE						
9	2	2	.	.	.	.
10	3	3	3	3	2	.
11	4	4	4	4	3	3
12	6	6	5	5	4	4
13	8	7	7	6	5	5
14	9	9	8	7	7	6
15	12	11	10	9	8	8
16	16	15	13	11	10	9
17	20	18	16	14	12	12
18	24	22	19	16	15	14
19	29	25	22	19	18	17
20	34	30	25	22	20	20
21	40	35	30	24	23	22
22	46	41	35	29	26	25
23	52	46	40	35	32	31
24	58	51	45	41	38	36
25	64	59	50	46	43	42
26	70	66	59	52	49	48
27	76	73	67	59	55	53
28	79	78	75	66	60	58
29	83	81	79	73	66	63
30	87	85	82	78	72	68
31	91	89	86	82	77	73
32	93	92	90	87	82	79
33	96	94	92	91	88	84
34	97	96	95	93	91	90
35	98	98	96	95	94	92
36	.	.	98	96	95	94
37	.	.	.	97	96	96
38	.	.	.	.	97	96
39	.	.	.	.	98	97
40	.	.	.	.	.	.
41	.	.	.	.	.	.

15.5	16.0	16.5	17.0	17.5	18.0
16.0	16.5	17.0	17.5	18.0	18.5
.	.	.	.	.	2
.	.	.	.	.	3
2	.	.	.	.	4
3	3	2	2	3	4
4	4	3	3	4	5
5	5	5	5	6	7
7	7	6	7	7	8
9	8	8	8	9	9
11	11	10	10	10	10
14	14	13	13	13	13
17	17	17	16	16	15
20	20	20	20	19	18
22	23	23	23	22	20
25	26	27	26	25	22
31	31	31	31	29	25
36	36	36	35	33	29
42	42	41	40	37	33
47	47	46	44	42	38
52	52	51	49	46	42
57	57	56	54	51	46
62	61	61	60	57	51
67	66	66	65	62	57
72	71	71	70	68	63
77	76	76	75	73	69
82	81	80	79	78	75
87	85	84	84	82	80
91	90	89	88	87	86
93	92	91	91	91	91
95	94	94	93	93	93
96	96	96	95	95	95
97	97	98	97	97	96
.	.	.	.	98	97
.	.	.	.	.	97

Table 11.5 Anthropometry Profiles for Ages 12 to 12.5 Years

PERCENTILE	3	10	25	50	75	90	97
WT (KG)	29.8	32.9	36.5	41.0	46.6	53.7	59.8
HT (CM)	138.0	142.4	147.2	151.7	156.7	160.5	164.9
SIHT (CM)	72.1	74.2	76.3	78.7	81.2	83.9	86.3
LELT (CM)	65.7	67.7	70.1	72.5	75.5	77.5	80.0
ACHT (CM)	111.0	114.9	118.7	123.0	127.4	131.0	134.7
TRLT (CM)	44.7	46.3	47.9	50.0	52.2	54.0	56.0
FALT (CM)	18.7	19.4	20.2	21.0	21.9	22.8	23.5
HELT (CM)	16.8	17.2	17.6	18.0	18.4	18.8	19.2
HEWI (CM)	13.2	13.5	13.7	14.1	14.4	14.7	15.0
BADI (CM)	28.8	29.8	30.7	32.0	33.1	34.2	35.5
CHWI (CM)	19.7	20.4	21.2	22.2	23.3	24.3	25.6
BCDI (CM)	20.5	21.4	22.3	23.4	24.7	25.7	27.2

BEHU (CM)	5.2	5.4	5.6	5.8	6.0	6.2	6.4
BIFE (CM)	7.4	7.7	7.9	8.2	8.4	8.7	9.0
HECI (CM)	50.5	51.3	52.1	53.0	54.0	54.9	55.9
UAFC (CM)	19.3	20.3	21.4	22.7	24.3	26.4	28.6
UAEC (CM)	18.0	18.9	20.0	21.2	22.9	25.0	27.3
FACI (CM)	18.2	18.9	19.7	20.6	21.6	23.0	24.2
CACI (CM)	25.9	27.2	28.3	29.9	31.7	33.6	35.7
THCI (CM)	39.2	41.0	43.3	46.0	49.4	53.4	57.8
TRSK (MM)	7.2	8.2	9.9	12.2	16.0	20.3	25.6
SSSK (MM)	4.9	5.5	6.3	7.7	10.5	16.3	23.0
BISK (MM)	3.5	4.1	5.1	6.5	8.4	11.2	14.9
SISK (MM)	4.2	5.1	6.4	8.6	12.5	18.5	27.7
CASK (MM)	6.6	8.1	10.2	13.2	17.7	23.8	30.5
SSK3 (MM)	17.7	20.4	24.0	28.9	38.6	54.8	72.8
SSK5 (MM)	29.1	33.3	39.9	49.1	64.4	88.1	116.2

Table 11.6 Motor Test and Physiology Profiles for Ages 12 to 12.5 Years

PROFILES MOTOR TESTS

PERCENTILE	3	10	25	50	75	90	97
FBA (N/1MIN)	27.1	22.4	18.2	13.9	10.1	6.9	4.3
PLT (N/20SEC)	54.3	60.3	65.3	70.4	75.6	80.0	85.2
SAR (CM)	9.7	14.1	18.1	22.1	26.6	30.3	33.5
VTJ (CM)	17.9	21.6	25.2	28.8	32.2	35.5	39.1
ARP (KG)	20.3	23.5	27.3	31.0	36.2	41.0	45.8
LEL (N/20SEC)	6.4	10.4	13.0	14.9	17.1	19.0	20.6
BAH (SEC)	0.0	0.3	3.9	7.8	14.8	23.9	34.9
SHR50 (SEC)	25.7	24.2	23.1	22.2	21.3	20.6	19.9
SHR480 (SEC)	193.6	180.2	170.4	162.5	154.4	148.8	142.4

PROFILES PHYSIOLOGY

PERCENTILE	3	10	25	50	75	90	97
PEFL (L/SEC)	2.4	3.4	4.5	5.4	6.5	7.6	8.5
FVCA (L)	1.5	1.8	2.1	2.4	2.8	3.2	3.6
FEV.5S (L)	0.6	1.0	1.4	1.6	1.9	2.1	2.4
FEV1S (L)	1.3	1.7	1.9	2.3	2.6	2.9	3.3
FEV3S (L)	1.5	1.8	2.1	2.4	2.8	3.2	3.5
PRRES (N/MIN)	123.8	113.1	101.2	91.3	82.8	75.5	69.0
PRREC (N/2MIN)	281.8	255.1	226.5	189.8	162.8	145.9	133.0

Besides individual comparisons, these charts can also be used to evaluate the mean dimensions and performances of a group of subjects with respect to the national standards. Such comparisons can provide useful information about the location of the average motor test results or body dimensions of a school class, a sports team, or any other group. Strong and average performances or small and large body dimensions can be detected, and conclusions can be drawn concerning teaching objectives and training programs.

These profile charts are useful diagnostic tools in evaluating body dimensions and motor test performances; however, they are to be used as screening devices. The interpretation of any profile should always be seen in its specific individual context.

Notes

[1]Norm scales were also constructed for all other anthropometric measurements, motor fitness tests, physiological measurements, and for skeletal maturity. Those interested may wish to address themselves to the editors.

[2]Profile charts for all age groups will be published in full very soon.

Chapter 12

Physical Activity: Movement Activities and Sport Participation

Roland Renson and Bart Vanreusel

Movement Activities of 6- to 12-Year-Old Girls

As explained in chapter 5, participation in movement activities by 6- to 12-year-old girls is estimated through their scores on two variables: (a) spatial stimulus for physical activities, and (b) material stimulus for physical activities through play equipment. Secondly, the involvement in movement activities is indicated by the global ESPA score (Environmental Stimulus for Physical Activity). The scores for spatial stimulus for engaging in physical activities are presented in Table 12.1. The scores for material stimulus for engaging in physical activities through play equipment are presented in Table 12.2.

A combination of all items of the movement activity inventory resulted in a variable called ESPA (Environmental Stimulus for Physical Activity). In Figure 12.1 the ESPA scores ranging from "very low" to "very high" are presented for each age group from 6 to 12 years. At 6 years, 48% of the girls show a low or very low physical activity stimulus. The percentage of girls with low stimulus scores decreases with increasing age. At the age of 12, only 15% of the girls show a low ESPA score (see Figure 12.1).

Only 2% of 6-year-old girls receive a high or very high stimulus for physical activities. This percentage gradually increases to 22% for the 12-year-old girls. The average ESPA score shows a similar tendency. It starts at 61.9 for the youngest girls, increases to 70.2 for girls of 9 years, to 75.4 for the oldest girls.

Figure 12.2 approaches the same data from a different angle. The frequency distributions for the different age groups are compiled within each ESPA category. The age tendency is clearly shown in these data. A gradual decrease of low ESPA scores with increasing age is matched by a gradual increase of high ESPA scores among older age groups. In general, the ESPA score can be described as a normally spread distribution from low to high within each age group. But from 6

Table 12.1 Spatial Stimulus for Physical Activity Among Girls From 6 to 12 Years

Spatial stimulus score	Age (years) 6		7		8		9		10		11		12	
	f	%	*f*	%	*f*	%	*f*	%	*f*	%	*f*	%	*f*	%
Low (8-10)	9	3	9	1	13	2	5	1	10	1	8	1	—	—
Rather low (11-13)	58	19	130	19	126	18	143	18	122	16	112	14	94	2
Average (14-16)	161	52	356	53	342	50	382	48	366	48	402	51	242	5
Rather high (17-19)	71	23	162	24	180	26	227	28	223	30	226	29	117	2
High (>19)	8	3	20	3	31	4	38	5	37	5	42	5	21	4
N	307	100	677	100	692	100	795	100	758	100	790	100	474	10
$\bar{X}$	15.2		15.2		15.4		15.6		15.6		15.7		15.5	

Table 12.2 Material Stimulus for Physical Activity Among Girls From 6 to 12 Years

Material stimulus score	Age (years) 6		7		8		9		10		11		12	
	f	%	*f*	%	*f*	%	*f*	%	*f*	%	*f*	%	*f*	%
Low (16)	5	2	13	2	15	1	8	1	6	1	6	1	2	0
Rather low (16-18)	86	28	166	25	124	18	147	18	138	18	125	16	89	19
Average (19-21)	132	43	309	46	303	46	361	46	322	43	334	42	199	42
Rather high (22-24)	74	24	164	24	217	31	240	30	243	32	269	34	148	31
High (>24)	9	3	24	3	33	5	37	5	49	6	56	7	36	8
N	306	100	676	100	692	100	793	100	758	100	790	100	474	100
$\bar{X}$	20.0		20.1		20.6		20.6		20.8		20.9		20.8	

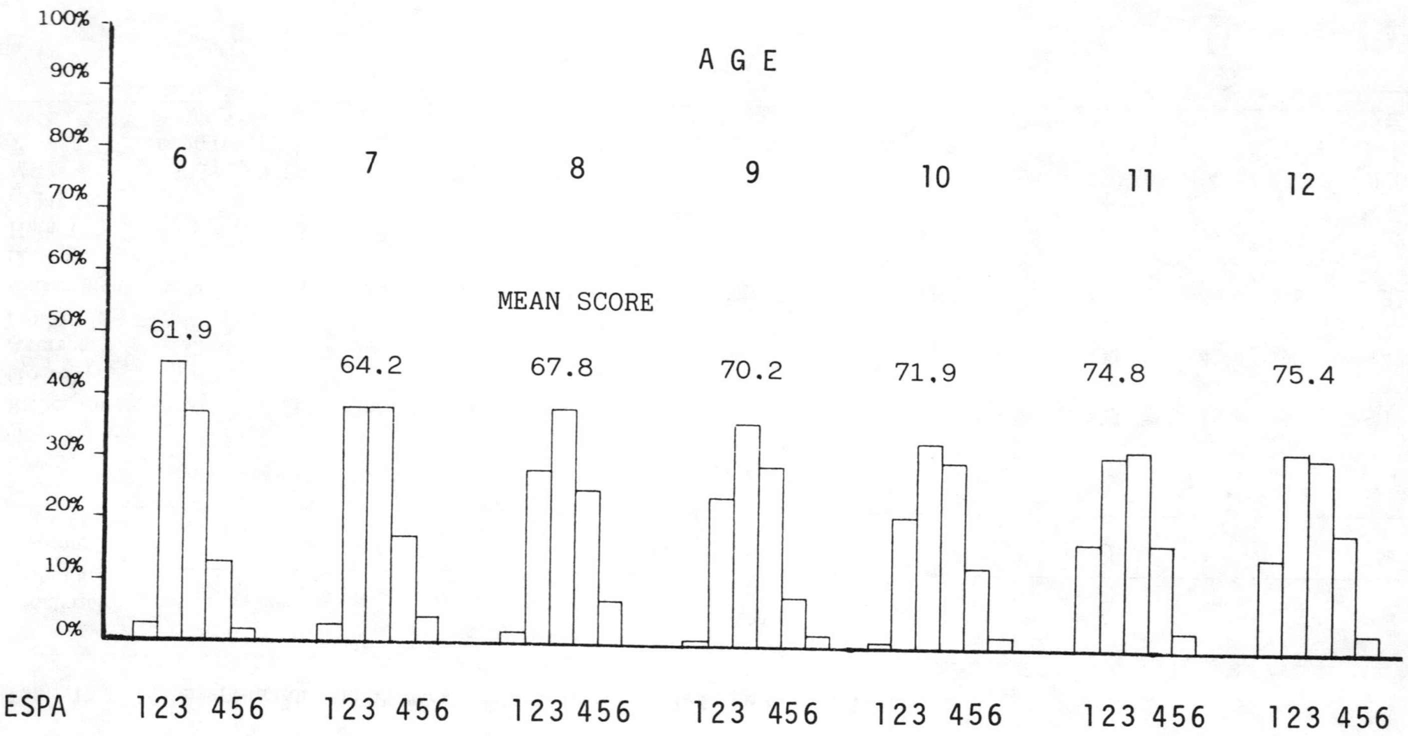

Figure 12.1. ESPA scores (Environmental Stimulus for Physical Activity) of 6- to 12-year-old girls. 1 = very low, 2 = low, 3 = rather low, 4 = rather high, 5 = high, 6 = very high.

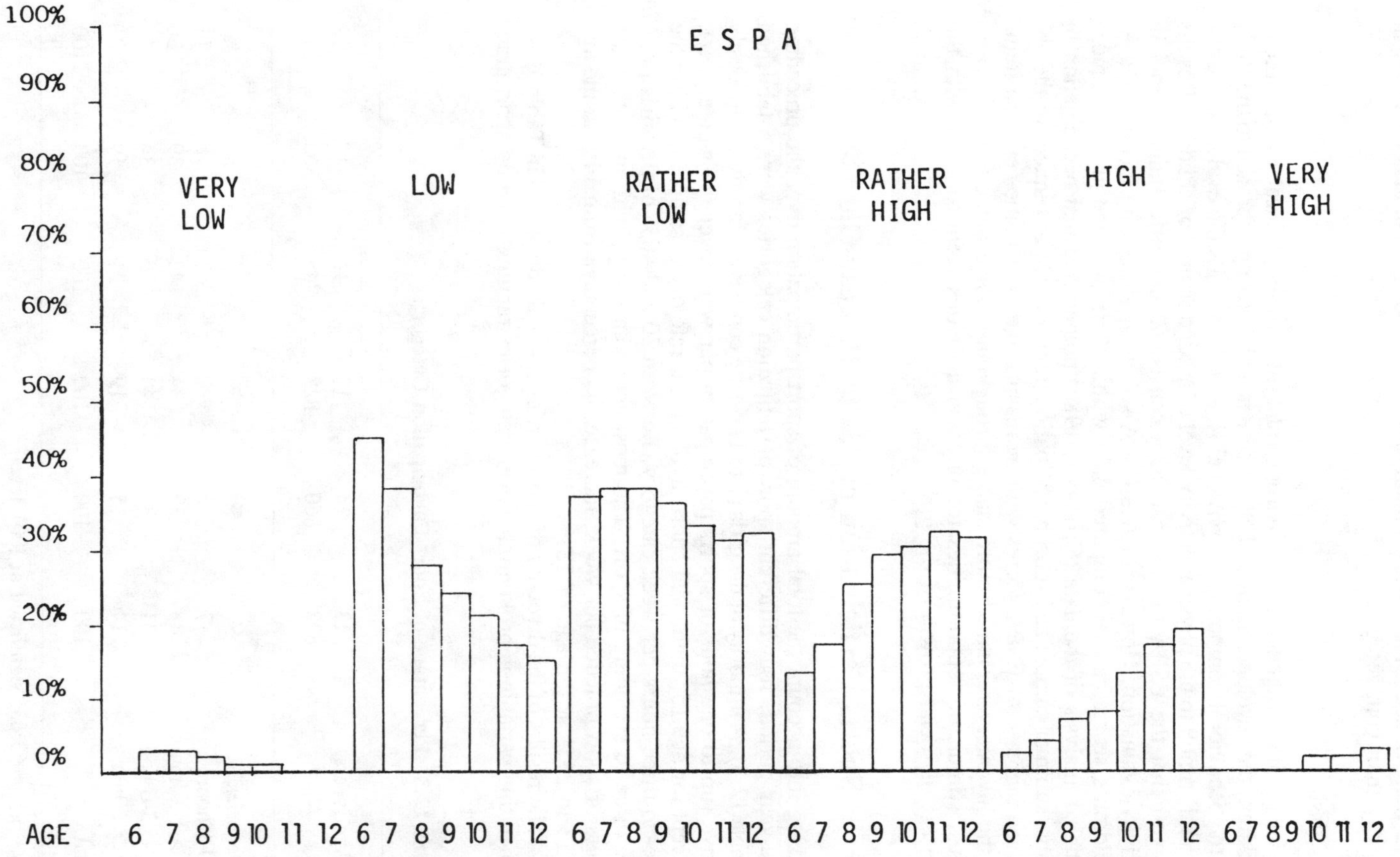

Figure 12.2. Percentages of ESPA categories (Environmental Stimulus for Physical Activity) of 6- to 12-year-old girls.

to 12 years of age, older girls gradually receive a stronger stimulus for physical activity than younger girls.

Discussion

By integrating different areas of environmental stimulus for physical activity among children, the development of an ESPA score is a globalizing approach to the study of the behavioral component of physical fitness. It permits the evaluation of the general stimuli to the physical activity level of a large sample of children. Results suggest that the ESPA method can be a consistent and differentiating tool in activity evaluation. However, since ESPA scores increase with increasing age, children's scores can be compared only within their own age group. A more detailed analysis of the data (Crombez, 1986) pointed out that participation in clubs, summer camps, and sport participation items mostly accounted for the observed increase of ESPA scores with increasing age. The home-centered items of the inventory remained more stable throughout the age range 6 to 12 years. Thus, stimulating opportunities for physical activities seem to grow with the process of social growth of the girls.

Sports Participation of 13- to 18-Year-Old Girls

Taking into account the total amount of sport participation over the preceding one-year period, four different sport participation categories were established (Table 12.3). A minority of the girls (7 to 11%) are completely inactive or modestly active (up to one hour of sports participation per week over the whole year). Except for age 15, the modal sport involvement rate of the sample is within the one- to three-hours-per-week category. Between 30 and 40% of the girls practice three to six hours of sport. The most active category, with more than six hours of sport practice per week, increases its percentage from 14% at the age of 13 to 21% at the age of 18.

The results of the diversity of sport participation are displayed in Table 12.4. When this variable is broken into seven categories ranging from no sport prac-

Table 12.3 Percentage of Sport Participation Categories

Age (years)	13	14	15	16	17	18
N	828	860	828	745	860	515
Categories	%	%	%	%	%	%
I: 0-1 hours	7	7	7	7	8	11
II: > 1-3 hours	48	39	34	42	39	36
III: > 3-6 hours	31	39	40	30	34	32
IV: > 6 hours	14	15	19	21	19	21
Total	100	100	100	100	100	100

Note. $\chi^2 = 63.63$, significant at .001 level.

Table 12.4 Percentage of Sport Participation Diversity

Age	13	14	15	16	17	18
N	828	860	828	745	860	515
Diversity (different sports)	%	%	%	%	%	%
0	2	2	1	2	1	3
1	6	6	8	8	8	7
2	46	34	30	26	24	24
3	27	30	26	23	24	20
4	11	14	15	17	17	19
5	5	8	9	12	14	13
> 6	3	6	11	12	12	14
Total	100	100	100	100	100	100

Note. $\chi^2 = 251.86$, significant at .001 level.

tice at all to more than six different sports, an increase in the sport diversity appears with age. These age differences in diversity are significant. Nevertheless, the highest frequency in all six age categories occurs among the girls participating in only two different sports.

Percentages of sport participation for each of the different sport activities are outlined in Table 12.5. The criterion for participation in a sport discipline was a minimum involvement of 10 min per week during the preceding one-year period.

Examining the general participation percentages, one notes that the two most practiced sports by far are gymnastics and swimming. Whereas gymnastics remains stable at about 90% participation rate, swimming shows a decline from 87% at age 13 to 71% at age 18. The latter is compensated for by a gradual increase in volleyball, track and field, tennis and basketball. Volleyball increases considerably from 10 to 46%, track and field from 12 to 26%, tennis from 13 to 21% and basketball triples its participation rate from 7 to 20%. Participation in table tennis, ice skating, cycling, dancing, and horseback riding remains fairly stable but low between 13 and 18 years, ranging between 5 and 12%. Walking, skiing, soccer, judo, other water sports (e.g., surfing), and other ball games (e.g., European handball) fluctuate between a minimal participation rate of 1 to 5%. These shifts in sport participation patterns are represented in Figure 12.3.

Examining the degree of formal sport affiliation of the girls, one finds the results in Table 12.5 show only judo, dancing, other water sports, other ball games, and soccer can be qualified as typical club sports (criterion: more than 50% club affiliation). However, these activities are engaged in by a minority of girls. Sports with moderately high club affiliation (criterion: 25 to 50% of the practitioners are club members) are horseback riding and tennis.

Among the two typical team games for girls, volleyball retains a fairly constant club membership rate (15 to 17%), whereas basketball sees its club membership drastically reduced from 23% at age 13 to 6% at 18 years. The latter also

Table 12.5 Percentages of Sport Participation for the Different Disciplines in General and in Club Context

Age	13		14		15		16		17		18	
N	828		860		828		745		860		515	
	%		%		%		%		%		%	
Sports	gen.	club	gen.	club	gen.	club	gen.	club	gen.	club	gen.	club
Gymnastics	91	11	92	9	92	9	92	7	91	6	90	6
Swimming	87	5	89	5	79	4	73	2	72	4	71	3
Volleyball	10	15	20	17	29	15	40	16	41	17	46	17
Track & field	12	25	16	17	21	14	23	10	24	9	26	8
Tennis	13	28	18	38	21	30	21	29	23	28	21	24
Basketball	7	23	11	16	18	14	18	7	18	12	20	6
Table tennis	7	12	8	9	9	11	12	7	12	12	12	6
Ice skating	8	10	11	3	9	4	8	7	6	8	4	5
Cycling	5	4	5	0	5	2	7	6	8	3	13	5
Dancing	6	72	6	53	5	76	6	50	6	60	8	68
Horseback	4	50	6	45	4	27	5	32	5	37	5	44
Walking	2	0	3	13	3	14	4	10	4	10	5	0
Skiing	2	11	2	11	2	18	3	22	4	15	3	27
Soccer	2	54	2	25	3	18	2	25	2	62	1	50
Judo	2	100	3	96	3	92	3	92	2	83	2	91
Other water sports	1	70	2	47	2	82	2	56	3	40	2	62
Other ball sports	1	43	1	29	1	50	1	60	2	62	2	50

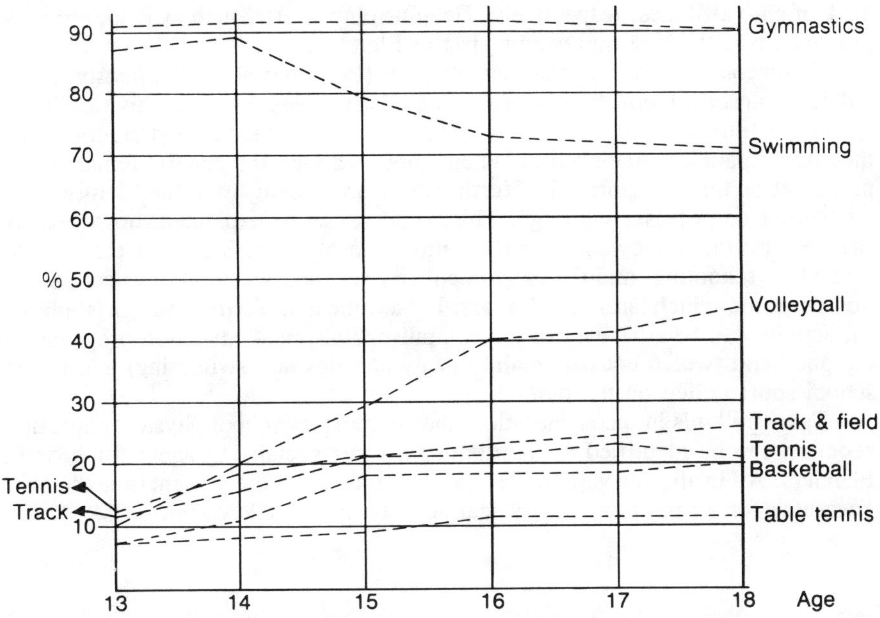

Figure 12.3. Participation changes in the sport disciplines according to age.

holds true for track and field, where club membership decreases from 25 to 8%. A most relevant observation is that the primary physical activities of Flemish girls, gymnastics and swimming, score definitely low on club affiliation.

Discussion

In contrast to the findings reported in the literature, the total amount of sport participation of Flemish girls increases relatively between the ages of 13 and 18. Whereas 55% of the 13-year-old girls practice sport less than 3 hours per week, 53% of the 17- and 18-year-olds practice more than 3 hours. Although the diversity in sport participation increases with age, the practice of only two different sports is the modal frequency for all age categories. Gymnastics and swimming, the two most predominant sports, are the classical physical education activities in the Belgian school curriculum.

The "minimal" physical education program in the Belgian school system varies between one and three lessons per week according to the school body. These lessons, however, account for the greatest part of female sport participation in general. This consideration gains even more support through the low percentages of club membership observed for these two activities. Volleyball, track and field, tennis, and basketball occupy the third to sixth position in the sporting hit parade. Except for tennis, these activities are the intramural and extramural school sports par excellence for girls. Both track and field and basketball suffer a considerable drop-out in their already limited number of club members between the ages of 13 and 18. Tennis and horseback riding count about 15 to

50% of club affiliates, respectively. Genuine club sports, such as judo, are only practiced by a trifling number of girls in Flanders.

When compared to their male counterparts (Renson et al., 1981; Renson et al., 1982), adolescent Flemish girls participate relatively less in sport activities. They spend less time on sports, they have a smaller variety in their sport practice, and they participate less in club life. When compared with the general female sport participation trends reported by North American investigators, the Flemish survey shows no decrease with age. This paradox can be explained, however, by two factors: (a) the low sport participation rate of Flemish girls at the start of secondary schooling, and (b) the compulsory secondary school physical education program, which lasts over 6 years. In fact, the major part of the girls' physical activity can be attributed to the compulsory physical education program on the one hand (which consists mainly of gymnastics and swimming) and to the school sport milieu on the other.

Taking all this into consideration, the compulsory school physical education program can be identified as the dominant sport socializing agent for girls in Flanders. All in all, this vulnerable ''protectorate'' is at the present time the only guarantee for a minimum of physical activity among adolescent girls.

Chapter 13

Summary

Gaston P. Beunen

The sociocultural background, growth, maturation, physical performance, and physical activities of girls aged 6 to 18 years are reported, based on a large representative sample of the Flemish population. As in previous studies on the physical fitness of Belgian youths (Ostyn et al., 1980; Beunen et al., 1988), physical fitness was defined as a conglomerate of somatic, motor, and behavioral components that can be studied from a developmental, differential, and sociocultural approach.

The selection of tests and measurements was based largely upon the previous project in which 21,174 examinations were made (Ostyn et al., 1980) and 588 boys were followed longitudinally between 12 and 19 years of age (Beunen et al., 1988). Moreover, a pilot study was conducted on girls of the same age levels in order to verify the objectivity, validity, and reliability of the tests and measurements for children and adolescents of the female sex.

The sample constitutes a good representation of the total school population of Flemish girls between 6 and 18 years. The girls stem largely from parents who have an educational level beyond the primary school level. The fathers occupy mainly working class positions (25%) or higher executive and managing functions, whereas only 25% of the mothers of the older girls are professionally active. About half of the sample lives in a semi-urban area, and only a relative minority lives in a rural area. The girls typically stem from two-children families. More than half of their mothers and about one third of their fathers never practiced any sport.

In general, all somatic dimensions increase throughout the entire period from 6 through 18 years. As the girls approach adulthood several dimensions level off and some even show a tendency to decline, such as suprailiac skinfold. Lengths, trunk breadths, and bone diameters increase linearly during childhood, show an increased growth during puberty, and gradually level off. All limb circumferences increase curvilinearly during childhood, accelerate, and then level off. All five skinfolds show a different growth pattern. During childhood the skinfolds increase or remain fairly stable, then increase and level off or even decline somewhat, such as suprailiac skinfold.

Skeletal maturation scores for the carpals and radius, ulna, and short bones (RUS) as assessed by the Tanner–Whitehouse technique increase curvilinearly during childhood. On the average the maximum score is reached at 12.5 years for the carpals and at 16 years for the RUS bones. The median age at menarche is 13.2 years according to the status quo method, and is slightly earlier, 12.9 years, for the retrospective method.

For several of the lung functions, cardiovascular characteristics, and motor performances similar growth patterns as those of somatic dimensions were observed. Contrary to what has been reported previously, a number of motor performance characteristics such as vertical jump, leg lifts, bent arm hang, plate tapping, and even shuttle run show a significant increase after 14 years.

Most trends observed in this large epidemiological study of Flemish girls correspond closely to what has been reported for other Caucasian populations. Medians for height of the often-quoted British sample never reach the same values as those of the Flemish girls. US girls are somewhat smaller until 13 years, after which the medians coincide exactly. Dutch girls have less weight for height, GB girls more weight for height, while US girls have identical weight for height to Flemish girls. The medians for height and weight of this sample correspond closely to those reported for a sample of more than 63,000 girls observed in the School Medical Centers of Flanders.

RUS and carpal bone scores of Flemish girls exceed those of British girls at all ages until late puberty. The median age at menarche for Flemish girls falls well within the range of medians/means from recent surveys in northwestern Europe. The secular decline in the median age at menarche occurred after World War II, and this trend seems to have stopped since the mid-1950s.

Norwegian girls have higher lung function characteristics than Flemish girls, whereas the blood pressures of Flemish girls and girls of the Fels Longitudinal Growth Study correspond closely. Flemish and Canadian girls have similar PWC170 values until 15.5 years, after which Canadian girls taper off in their performance capacity and Flemish girls further increase their capacity.

Flemish and Dutch girls perform equally well in static strength, but Flemish girls have much less explosive strength (vertical jump) than their Dutch age peers. Also, for functional strength (bent arm hang) Dutch girls perform better than Flemish girls, who perform equally as well as American girls. The trend toward a significant increase in performance after 14 years is also observed for some motor characteristics in recent reports on motor performance and probably reflects a change in lifestyle in adolescent girls.

The participation in movement activities of 6- to 12-year-old girls is estimated through their scores on a spatial stimulus for physical activities, a material stimulus for physical activities, and a global environmental stimulus for physical activities. In general the global environmental stimulus score is normally distributed within each age category, but older girls receive a stronger stimulus for physical activity than younger girls. For girls in the age range 13 to 18 years, the total amount of sports participation and diversity in participation was observed. Between 30 and 40% of the girls practice 3 to 6 hours of sport per week. The most active category, with more than 6 hours of sport practice per week, increases from 14% at the age of 13 years to 21% at the age of 18 years. Also the sport diversity increases with age. The two most practiced sports by far are gymnastics and swimming, and these are typically school sports. This implies that the major part of the girls' physical activity must be attributed to the compulsory physical education program on the one hand and to the school sport milieu on the other hand. The compulsory school physical education program can thus be identified as the dominant sport socializing agent for girls in Flanders.

In conclusion, the present monograph gives a fairly good account of the fitness of Flemish girls; fitness interpreted in a broad sense rather than a more narrow sense, as is the case for the "Health-related fitness" concept that has emerged quite recently. If health is viewed not only as the absence of disease and injuries, but as a physical, social, and psychological well-being, then the components discussed herein are an essential part of physical well being since they enhance a more optimal functioning of the human being. It is with satisfaction that we see that our studies on the physical fitness of Belgian youths have largely contributed to the establishment of the Eurofit test battery, which in turn has led to the recommendation by the Committee of Ministers of the European Council to propagate this test battery in all countries of the European Council (Council of Europe, Committee for the Development of Sport, 1988).

Appendix A

Menarche questionnaire

a. Do you know about menstruation?

yes:
no:

b. Did you already have a menstrual period?

yes:
no:

c. If yes, when did you have your first menstrual period?
year:
season: Winter, Spring, Summer, Fall (underline)
month: Jan, Feb, Mar, Apr, May, Jun, Jul, Aug, Sep, Oct, Nov, Dec (underline)

d. If possible, give the exact date:
day:
month:
year:

References

American Alliance for Health, Physical Education, and Recreation. (1976). *Youth fitness test manual*. Reston, VA: Author.

Asmussen, E. (1973). Growth in muscular strength and power. In G.L. Rarick (Ed.), *Physical activity: Human growth and development* (pp. 60-79). New York: Academic Press.

Beckers, R., & Pleysier, R. (1980). *Analyse anthropométrique effectuée auprès des miliciens belges: Levéé 1979*. Bruxelles: Ministère de la Santé Publique et de la Famille.

Beckers, R., & Pleysier, R. (1982a). *Analyse anthropométrique de la population scolaire belges 1980-1981*. Bruxelles: Ministère de la Santé Publique et de la Famille.

Beckers, R., & Pleysier, R. (1982b). *Antropometrische analyse van de Belgische schoolbevolking, 1980-1981* (pp. 20-22). Brussel: Ministerie van Volksgezondheid en het Gezin.

Bergsten-Brucefors, A. (1976). A note on the accuracy of recalled age at menarche. *Annals of Human Biology*, **3**, 71-73.

Beunen, G., & Cameron, N. (1980). The reproducibility of TW2 skeletal age assessments by a self-taught assessor. *Annals of Human Biology*, **7**, 155-162.

Beunen, G., & Malina, R.M. (1988). Growth and physical performance relative to the timing of the adolescent spurt. *Exercise and Sport Science Reviews*, **16**, 503-540.

Beunen, G.P., Malina, R.M., Van't Hof, M.A., Simons, J., Ostyn, M., Renson, R., & Van Gerven, D. (1988). *Adolescent growth and motor performance: A longitudinal study of Belgian boys*. HKP Sport Science Monograph Series. Champaign, IL: Human Kinetics.

Beunen, G., Simons, J., Ostyn, M., Renson, R., Van Gerven, D., Claessens, A., Vanreusel, B., Colla, R., & Schueremans, C. (1982). Le 'Leuven Growth Study of Flemish Girls'. In J. Simons, R. Renson, & H. Levarlet-Joye (Eds.), *Projet de l'étude et controle de la qualité des données* (pp. 59-75). Leuven, Belgium: Instituut voor Lichamelijke Opleiding.

Beunen, G., Van Gerven, D., & Vanden Eynde, B. (1977). Reliability of three cardiorespiratory field tests. In H. Lavallée & R. Shephard (Eds.), *Frontiers of activity and child health* (pp. 75-81). Québec: Pélican.

Beunen, G., & Van Hellemont, A. (1980). Body structure and somatotype in physical education students. *Anthropologiai Közlemenyek*, **24**, 15-21.

Boas, F. (1892) The growth of children. *Science*, **19-20**, 256-257, 281-282, 351-352.

Bouchard, C., Thibault, M.-C., & Jobin, J. (1981). Advances in selected areas of human work physiology. *Yearbook of Physical Anthropology*, **24**, 1-36.

Bovend'eerdt, J.H.F., Bermink, M.J.E., van Hijfte, T., Ritmeester, J.W., Kemper, H.C.G., & Verschuur, R. (1980). *De MOPER fitness test: Onderzoeksverslag*. Haarlem: De Vrieseborch.

Branta, C., Haubenstricker, J., & Seefeldt, V. (1984). Age changes in motor skills during childhood and adolescence. *Exercise and Sport Science Reviews*, **12**, 467-520.

Cameron, N. (1978). The methods of auxological anthropometry. In F. Falkner & J.M. Tanner (Eds.), *Human growth: Vol. 2. Postnatal growth* (pp. 35-90). London: Ballière Tindall.

Cameron, N. (1984). *The measurement of human growth*. London: Croom Helm.

Canadian Association for Health, Physical Education and Recreation. (1968). *The physical work capacity of Canadian children aged 7 to 17*. Ottawa, ON: Author.

Canadian Association for Health, Physical Education and Recreation. (1980). *Fitness performance II: Test manual*. Ottawa, ON: Author.

Carter, J.E.L. (1975). *The Heath-Carter somatotype method*. San Diego: San Diego State University.

Cliquet, R. (1963). *Bijdrage tot de kennis van het verband tussen de sociale status en een aantal antropobiologische kenmerken* [Contribution to the knowledge of the relationship between social status and a series of anthropobiological characteristics]. Brussels: Paleis der Academiën.

Cotes, J.E. (1979). *Long function: Assessment and application in medicine*. Oxford: Blackwell.

Cotes, J.E., Dobbs, J.M., Hall, A.M., Heywood, C., & Laurence, K.M. (1979). Sitting height, fat-free mass and body fat as reference variables for lung function in healthy British children: Comparison with stature. *Annals of Human Biology*, **6**, 307-314.

Council of Europe, Committee for the Development of Sport. (1988). *Eurofit: European test of physical fitness*. Rome: Author.

Crombez, C. (1986). *Spelstimuli bij meisjes uit het basisonderwijs* [Play stimulus among primary school girls]. Unpublished licentiate thesis, Catholic University of Leuven, Leuven, Belgium.

Cronk, C.E., & Roche, A.F. (1982). Race- and sex-specific reference data for triceps and subscapular skinfolds and weight/stature. *The American Journal of Clinical Nutrition*, **35**, 347-354.

Danker-Hopfe, H. (1986). Menarcheal age in Europe. *Yearbook of Physical Anthropology*, **29**, 81-112.

De Roover, M. (1982). *Consistentie-onderzoek van een vragenlijst over spelactiviteiten bij leerlingen uit het lager onderwijs* [Analysis of consistency of a questionnaire on play activities among primary school girls]. Unpublished licentiate thesis, Catholic University of Leuven, Leuven, Belgium.

Duckworth, W.J.H. (1912). *The international agreement for the unification of anthropometric measurements to be made on the living subject*. Cambridge: Cambridge University Press.

Dupertuis, C.W., & Tanner, J.M. (1950). The pose of the subject for photogrammetric anthropometry, with special reference to somatotyping. *American Journal of Physical Anthropology*, **7**, 27-48.

Espenschade, A. (1960). Motor development. In W.R. Johnson (Ed.), *Science and medicine of exercise and sports* (pp. 419-439). New York: Harper.

Eveleth, P.B., & Tanner, J.M. (1976). *Worldwide variation in human growth*. Cambridge: Cambridge University Press.

Faust, M.S. (1977). Somatic development of adolescent girls. *Monograph of the Society for Research in Child Development*, **42**(Serial No. 169).

Finney, D.J. (1952). *Probit analysis*. Cambridge: Cambridge University Press.

Gasser, T., Köhler, W., Müller, H.-G., Kneip, A., Largo, R., Molinari, L., & Prader, A. (1984). Velocity and acceleration of height growth using kernel estimation. *Annals of Human Biology*, **11**, 397-411.

Goldstein, H. (1978). Sampling for growth studies. In F. Falkner & J.M. Tanner (Eds.), *Human growth. Volume 1. Principles and prenatal growth* (pp. 183-208). New York: Plenum.

Greulich, W.W., & Pyle, S.I. (1966). *Radiographic atlas of skeletal development of the hand and wrist*. Stanford, California: Stanford University Press.

Guyda, H.J. (1986). Hormonal regulation of growth at puberty. In A. Demirjian (Ed.), *Human growth: A multidisciplinary review* (pp. 203-212). London: Taylor and Francis.

Hamill, P.V.V., Drizd, T.A., Johnson, C.L., Reed, R.B., & Roche, A.F. (1977). NCHS Growth curves for children birth-18 years. *Vital Health Statistics* (Series 11-165). Rockville, MD: U.S. Department of Health, Education and Welfare.

Haubenstricker, J.L., & Seefeldt, V.D. (1986). Acquisition of motor skills during childhood. In V. Seefeldt (Ed.), *Physical activity and well-being* (pp. 41-102). Reston, VA: AAHPERD.

Hoge Raad voor de Statistiek. (1967). Typologie van de gemeenten naar de graad van verstedelijking [Typology of municipalities according to their degree of urbanization]. *Statistisch Jaarboek*, **46**, 40-54.

Jeurissen, A. (1969). L'âge au moment des premières règles et son évolution en Belgique au cours des quarante dernières années. *Acta Paediatrica Belgica*, **23**, 219-330.

Johnston, F.E., Hamill, P.V.V., & Lemeshow, S. (1972). *Skinfold thickness of children 6-11 years* (DHEW Publication No. 73-1602 HSM). Rockville, MD: U.S. Department of Health, Education and Welfare.

Johnston, F.E., Hamill, P.V.V., & Lemeshow, S. (1974). *Selected body measurements of children 6-11 years* (DHEW Publication No. 73-1605 HSM). Rockville, MD: U.S. Department of Health, Education and Welfare.

Jones, H.E. (1949). *Motor performance and growth: A developmental study of static dynamometric strength*. Berkeley: University of California Press.

Kemper, H.C.G., & Verschuur, R. (1985a). Motor performance fitness tests. In H.C.G. Kemper (Ed.), *Growth, health and fitness of teenagers* (pp. 96-106). Basel: Karger.

Kemper, H.C.G., & Verschuur, R. (1985b). Other functions. In H.C.G. Kemper (Ed.), *Growth, health and fitness of teenagers* (pp. 127-136). Basel: Karger.

Knops, J., & Van Landeghem, H. (1969). Menarche-leeftijd van een Leuvense bevolking. *Nota's over Schoolgezondheidszorg*, **5**, 12-15.

Krahenbuhl, G.S., Skinner, J.S, & Kohrt, W.M. (1985). Developmental aspects of maximal aerobic power in children. *Exercise and Sports Science Reviews*, **13**, 503-538.

Lange-Andersen, K., Rutenfranz, J., Seliger, V., Ilmarinen, J., Berndt, I., Kylian, H., & Ruppel, M. (1984). The growth of lung volumes affected by physical performance capacity in boys and girls during childhood and adolescence. *European Journal of Applied Physiology*, **52**, 380-384.

Lindgren, G. (1976). Height, weight and menarche in Swedish urban school children in relation to socio-economic and regional factors. *Annals of Human Biology*, **3**, 501-528.

Lohman, T.G. (1981). Skinfolds and body density and their relation to body fatness: A review. *Human Biology*, **53**, 181-225.

Malina, R.M. (1974). Adolescent changes in size, build, composition and performance. *Human Biology*, **46**, 117-131.

Malina, R.M. (1978). Adolescent growth and maturation: Selected aspects of current research. *Yearbook of Physical Anthropology*, **21**, 63-94.

Malina, R.M. (1986a). Physical growth and maturation. In V. Seefeldt (Ed.), *Physical activity and well-being*. Reston, VA: AAHPERD.

Malina, R.M. (1986b). Growth of muscle tissue and muscle mass. In F. Falkner & J.M. Tanner (Eds.), *Human growth. Volume 2. Postnatal growth, neurobiology* (pp. 77-99). New York: Plenum.

Malina, R.M., & Roche, A.F. (1983). *Manual of physical status and performance in childhood: Volume 2. Physical performance*. New York: Plenum.

Meredith, H.V. (1981). An addendum on presence and abscence in a midgrowth spurt in somatic dimensions. *Annals of Human Biology*, **8**, 473-476.

Merni, F., Balboni, M., Bargellini, S., & Menegatti, G. (1981). Differences in males and females in joint movement range during growth. In J. Borms, M. Hebbelinck & A. Venerando (Eds.), *The female athlete* (pp. 168-175). Basel: Karger.

Mocellin, R., Rutenfranz, J., & Singer, R. (1971). Zur Frage von Normwerten der körperlichen Leistungsfähigkeit (W170) im Kindes und Jugendalter. *Zeitschrift für Kinderheilkunde*, **110**, 140-165.

Ostyn, M., Simons, J., Beunen, G., Renson, R., & Van Gerven, D. (Eds.) (1980). *Somatic and motor development of Belgian secondary schoolboys. Norms and standards*. Leuven, Belgium: Leuven University Press.

Pauwels, J.M. (1977). Fertigkeitsdimensionen für den Umgang mit dem Ball. Eine Faktoranalyse mit Daten 12 bis 19-jährigen Jungen bezüglich ihres Fertigkeitsniveaus im Basketball, Fussball, Volleyball und Handball. In R. Bauss & K. Roth (Eds.), *Motorische Entwicklung*. Darmstadt, Bundesrepublik Deutschland: Institut für Sportwissenschaft, T.H.D.

Renson, R. (1973). *Sociokulturele determinanten van de somatische ontwikkeling, de motorische vaardigheid en het sportgedrag van 13-jarige Belgische jongens* [Socioculture determinants of the somatic development, motor fitness and sport behavior of 13-year-old Belgian boys]. Unpublished doctoral dissertation, Catholic University of Leuven, Leuven, Belgium.

Renson, R. (1975). Sociocultural determinants of the physical fitness of 13 year old Belgian boys. *Hermes*, **19**, 349-367.

Renson, R., Beunen, G., De Witte, L., Ostyn, M., Simons, J., & Van Gerven, D. (1980). The social spectrum of the physical fitness of 12- to 19-year-old boys. In M. Ostyn, G. Beunen & J. Simons (Eds.), *Kinanthropometry II*. International Series on Sport Sciences, 9 (pp. 104-118). Baltimore: University Park Press.

Renson, R., Beunen, G., Ostyn, M., Simons, J., Swalus, P., & Van Gerven, D. (1978). Sociocultural differentiation of physical fitness of preadolescent Belgian boys. In R.J. Shephard & H. Lavallee (Eds.), *Physical fitness assessment: Principles, practice and application* (pp. 248-256). Springfield, IL: Charles C Thomas.

Renson, R., Beunen, G., Ostyn, M., Simons, J., Uyttebrouck, J., Van Gerven, D., & Vanreusel, B. (1981). Differentiation of physical fitness in function of sport participation. *Hermes*, **15**, 435-444.

Renson, R., Beunen, G., Ostyn, M., Simons, J., & Van Gerven, D. (1980). Soziale Bedingungen der Physical Fitness. In K. Willimczik & M. Grosser (Eds.), *Die motorische Entwicklung im Kindes- und Jugendalter* (Schriftenreihe BISP 24) (pp. 353-366). Schorndorf: Hofman.

Renson, R., Beunen, G., Ostyn, M., Simons, J., Van Gerven, D., & Vanreusel, B. (1982). Family constellation and sport participation of 12 to 19 year old Belgian boys. In L. Bollaert & P. De Knop (Eds.), *Family sport and leisure* (pp. 133-160). Brussels: Free University of Brussels.

Renson, R., Beunen, G., Van Gerven, D., Simons, T., & Ostyn, M. (1980). Description of motor ability tests and anthropometric measurements. In M. Ostyn, T. Simons, G. Beunen, R. Renson, & D. Van Gerven, *Somatic and Motor Development of Secondary Schoolboys. Norms and Standards* (pp. 24-44). Leuven, Leuven University Press.

Rivet, P. (1912). Entente internationale pour l'unification des mesures anthropométriques sur le vivant. *L'Anthropologie*, **23**, 623-627.

Roberts, J., & Maurer, K. (1977). *Blood pressure level of persons 6-74 years: United States, 1971-1974* (Public Service HRA Publication No. 78-1648). Washington, DC: U.S. Department of Health, Education and Welfare.

Roche, A.F., Eichorn, D., McCammon, R.W., Reed, R.B., Valadian, I., Himes, J.H., Kent, R.L. Jr., & Siervogel, R.M. (1979). The natural history of blood pressure. Final report on contract No. 1-HV-42985 reported in R.M. Malina & A.F. Roche (1983). *Manual of physical status and performance in childhood. Volume 2. Physical performance*. New York: Plenum.

Roche, A.F., Mukherjee, D., & Guo, S. (1986). Head circumference growth patterns: Birth to 18 years. *Human Biology*, **58**, 893-906.

Roche, A.F., Mukherjee, D., Guo, S., & Moore, W.M. (1987). Head circumference reference data: Birth to 18 years. *Pediatrics*, **79**, 706-712.

Roede, M.J., & Van Wieringen, J.C. (1985). Growth diagrams 1980. Netherlands third nation-wide survey. *Tijdschrift voor Sociale Gezondheidszorg*, (Suppl. 63), 1-34.

Safrit, M.S. (1973). *Evaluation in physical education. Assessing motor behavior*. Englewood Cliffs, NJ: Prentice Hall.

SAS Institute. (1982). *SAS user's guide: Statistics*. Cary, NC: Author.

SAS Institute. (1985). *SAS/graph user's guide*. Cary, NC: Author.

Sheldon, W.H., Lewis, N.D.C., & Tenney, A.M. (1969). Psychiatric patterns and physical constitutions. In D.V.S. Sankar (Ed.), *Schizophrenia: Current concepts and research* (pp. 838-912). Hicksville, NY: PJD Publications.

Shephard, R.J. (1978). *Human physiological work capacity*. Cambridge: Cambridge University Press.

Shuttleworth, F.K. (1937). Sexual maturation and the physical growth of girls aged six to nineteen. *Monographs of the Society for Research in Child Development*, **2**(Serial No. 12).

Siegel, S., & Castellan, N.J. (1988). *Nonparametric statistics for the behavioral sciences*. New York: McGraw-Hill.

Simons, J., Beunen, G., Ostyn, M., Renson, R., Swalus, P., Van Gerven, D., & Willems, E. (1968-1969). Factor-analysen van de physical fitness van 12-tot 19-jarige jongens uit het middelbaar onderwijs. *Werken Belgische Geneeskundige Vereniging Lichamelijke Opvoeding en Sport*, **21**, 57-73.

Simons, J., Beunen, G., Ostyn, M., Renson, R., Swalus, P., Van Gerven, D., & Willems, E. (1969). Construction d'une batterie de tests d'aptitude motrice pour garçons de 12 à 19 ans par la méthode de l'analyse factorielle. *Kinanthropologie*, **1**, 323-362.

Simons, J., Beunen, G., Ostyn, M., Renson, R., Swalus, P., Van Gerven, D., & Willems, E. (1970). Constructie van een motorische testbatterij voor jongens van 12 tot 19 jaar door middel van faktoranalysen. *Sport*, **12**, 2-21.

Simons, J., Ostyn, M., Beunen, G., Renson, R., Van Gerven, D. (1978). Factor analytic study of motor ability of Belgian girls, age 12 to 19. In F. Landry & W.A.R. Orban (Eds.), *Biomechanics of sports and kinanthropometry* (pp. 395-401). Miami: Symposia Specialists.

Simons, J., & Renson, R. (1982). *Evaluation of motor fitness*. Council of Europe: Committee for the Development of Sport.

Simons, J., & Van Gerven, D. (1970-1971). De dimensies van de lichaamsstruktuur volgens de factoranalysemethode. *Werken Belgische Geneeskundige Vereniging Lichamelijke Opvoeding en Sport*, **22B**, 45-52.

Smith, P.L. (1979). Splines as a useful and convenient statistical tool. *American Statistician*, **33**, 57-62.

Tanner, J.M. (1951). Some notes on the reporting of growth data. *Human Biology*, **23**, 93-159.

Tanner, J.M. (1962). *Growth at adolescence* (2nd ed.). Oxford: Blackwell.

Tanner, J.M. (1978). *Foetus into man: Physical growth from conception to maturity*. London: Open Books.

Tanner, J.M., & Cameron, N. (1980). Investigation of the mid-growth spurt in height, weight and limb circumference in single-year velocity data from the London 1966-67 growth survey. *Annals of Human Biology*, **7**, 565-577.

Tanner, J.M., Hughes, P.C.R., & Whitehouse, R.H. (1981). Radiographically determined widths of bone muscle and fat in the upper arm and calf from age 3-18 years. *Annals of Human Biology*, **8**, 495-517.

Tanner, J.M., & Whitehouse, R.H. (1975). Revised standards for triceps and subscapular skinfolds in British children. *Archives of Disease in Childhood*, **50**, 142-145.

Tanner, J.M., & Whitehouse, R.H. (1976). Clinical longitudinal standards for height, weight, height velocity and weight velocity and the stages of puberty. *Archives of Disease in Childhood*, **51**, 170-179.

Tanner, J.M., Whitehouse, R.H., Cameron, N., Marshall, W.A., Healy, M.J.R., & Goldstein, H. (1983). *Assessment of skeletal maturity and prediction of adult height (TW2-method)*. London: Academic Press.

Tanner, J.M., Whitehouse, R.H., Marshall, W.A., Healy, M.J.R., & Goldstein, H. (1975). *Assessment of skeletal maturity and prediction of adult height (TW2-method)*. London: Academic Press.

Tanner, J.M., Whitehouse, R.H., & Takaishi, M. (1966). Standards from birth to maturity for height, weight, height velocity, and weight velocity. *Archives of Disease in Childhood*, **41**, 454-471, 613-635.

Van Den Bosch, A. (1979). *Pattern-card of Flemish schools*. Unpublished manuscript, National Secretariat for Education, Brussels.

Van Gerven, D. (1976). De dimensies van de lichaamsstruktuur volgens de faktor-analyse mehode op een groep van 335 preadolescenten. *Hermes*, **10**, 83-95.

Van Gerven, D., & Vanden Eynde, B. (1978). Factor analysis of three cardiorespiratory tests within a group of male and female secondary school students. In F. Landry & W.A.R. Orban (Eds.), *Biomechanics of sports and kinanthropometry* (pp. 403-407). Miami: Symposia Specialists.

Vanreusel, B. (1985). *Tijdstrendanalyse van sportdeelnamestijlen* [Time trend analysis of sport participation styles]. Unpublished doctoral dissertation, Catholic University of Leuven, Leuven, Belgium.

Vercauteren, M., & Susanne, C. (1984). Untersuchungen über das gegenwartige Menarchealter in Belgien. *Anthropologischer Anzeiger*, **52**, 211-217.

Vercauteren, M., Susanne, C., & Orban, R. (1984). Secular evolution in Brussels between 1960 and 1980. In T. Boems, A. Sonit, C. Susanne, & M. Hebbelinck (Eds.), *Human growth and development* (pp. 215-223). New York: Plenum.

Wellens, R. (1984). The influence of sociocultural variables and sports participation on the age at menarche of Flemish girls. Unpublished master's thesis, the University of Texas at Austin, Austin, Texas.

Woynarowska, B., Mukherjee, D., Roche, A.F., & Siervogel, R.M. (1985). Blood pressure changes during adolescence and subsequent adult blood pressure level. *Hypertension*, **7**, 695-701.

